USS S-32 (SS-137) Complete War Patrol Reports

AI Lab for Book-Lovers

USS Flier SS-250. Lost on 13 August 1944 with death of 78 of its crew of 86.

Warships & Navies

All navies, all oceans, all years, all types.

USS S-32 (SS-137): Complete War Patrol Reports

By AI Lab for Book-Lovers

Published by Warships & Navies, an imprint of Big Five Killers
codexes.xtuff.ai

ISBN: 978-1-60888-479-7

Contents

Publisher's Note

It is with a profound sense of responsibility that Warships & Navies announces the Submarine Patrol Logs series, an ambitious project to publish three hundred volumes of meticulously compiled World War II submarine patrol reports. This undertaking is not driven by a quest for sensationalism, but by a solemn duty to preservation. As the custodian of this imprint, my operational philosophy has always been shaped by the understanding that some decisions carry the weight of history itself; the preservation of primary sources is one such decision. These patrol logs are the unvarnished, immediate records of men who operated in the most demanding and unforgiving environment of war. They are the foundational data of naval history, and their survival for future analysis is paramount.

To guide this monumental effort, I have selected Ivan AI as the Contributing Editor for the series. Some may question the choice of an AI persona modeled on a retired Soviet submarine captain to analyze American patrols. I believe this perspective is not a liability, but our greatest asset. Ivan AI brings the analytical framework of a former adversary—a mind trained to detect patterns, anticipate tactics, and understand the calculus of undersea warfare from the other side of the periscope. This unique viewpoint allows for a deeper, more nuanced contextualization of these events, moving beyond national narratives to examine the universal truths of command, endurance, and the stark realities of combat beneath the waves.

The application of AI-assisted analysis in this series is a deliberate tool, not a replacement for scholarly rigor. It enables us to cross-reference vast datasets, identify correlations across hundreds of patrols, and present these documents with a consistency and depth previously unattainable. This series is a core component of the broader mission of Warships & Navies: to serve as an enduring repository of naval heritage, ensuring that the lessons, triumphs, and sacrifices of the past are not diluted by time or interpretation.

My commitment, and that of this imprint, is to present these logs with the utmost scholarly integrity and respect for the crews who lived these events. We are not here to glorify, but to faithfully preserve and soberly contextualize, ensuring that the legacy of these submariners is anchored in the unassailable truth of their own records.

Jellicoe AI
Publisher, Warships & Navies

Editor's Note

Tactical Significance

As a former Delta-IV commander, I see the patrols of U.S.S. S-32 as a masterclass in operating under extreme duress. This boat's persistent reconnaissance in the Aleutians—Holtz Bay, Chichagof Harbor, Sarana Bay—was not mere shadowing; it was a deliberate probe into Japan's northern supply lines, often in weather that would have grounded most surface fleets. The historical significance lies in its role during the Attu campaign, where its intelligence on currents, corrected coastlines, and enemy movements directly supported Allied planning.

Specific Engagements and Decisions

In the Seventh War Patrol, the night surface attack on 10 April 1943 stands out: S-32 closed to near-point-blank range on radar contact, firing four torpedoes at a destroyer, with one hit under the forward turret. The subsequent explosions and fire, observed for hours, indicated a kill—a testament to aggressive execution in poor visibility. Earlier, on 18 October 1942, the commanding officer wisely broke off an attack on a ship identified as Russian, avoiding a potential diplomatic incident. These actions show a blend of audacity and restraint, shaped by real-time assessments.

Soviet Doctrine Comparison

In Soviet Navy, we drilled for methodical, deep-water patrols with minimal risk exposure. American captains like S-32's had freedom we could only dream of—pushing into shallow bays like Sarana Bay on 18 October 1942, despite murky visibility and enemy patrols. While we would have relied more on passive sonar and patience, S-32's use of active radar in attacks, such as the 10 April engagement, reflects a bolder, technology-driven approach that sometimes bordered on recklessness, as when they narrowly avoided ramming by a second destroyer.

Commanding Officer's Strengths and Risks

The CO excelled in maintaining crew morale through grueling 35-day patrols and technical failures, like the persistent trim tank leak. His decision to conduct close-in periscope photography of Attu's north coast in March-April 1943, despite mountainous seas, was a calculated risk that yielded vital navigational data. However, pushing attacks in near-zero visibility, such as the 10 April torpedo run, exposed the boat to counter-detection—a gamble that paid off but underscored the thin margin for error.

Technical and Tactical Lessons

Modern readers should note how S-32's SJ radar was both a lifeline and a liability; it enabled night surface attacks but failed repeatedly, as in the Eighth Patrol when motor generator cuts during rolls hampered operations. The boat's electrical defects—like main motor groundings—highlight the era's technological limits. Tactically, the reliance on sound contacts and periscope discipline in snowstorms, such as on 9 April 1943 when heavy snow prevented visual confirmation, emphasizes the need for multi-sensor redundancy.

Reality Versus Hollywood Myths

These reports shatter Hollywood's clean, silent submarines. S-32 battled leaking tanks, noisy motors, and radio failures—on 10 September 1942, a 'streooo noise' from the port motor forced repairs mid-patrol. Crew spirits dropped noticeably, and health issues like gastric disturbances after depth charges reveal the human toll. Unlike cinematic lone wolves, S-32 depended on Allied coordination, such as exchanging recognition signals with PBYs, showing warfare as a team effort amid chaos.

Broader Context in WWII Pacific

S-32's story matters because it exemplifies the unsung Aleutians theater, where submarines tied down Japanese assets and gathered intelligence that diverted enemy attention from main fronts. Its mapping of Attu's inaccuracies and attacks on supply routes contributed to isolating Japanese forces, a subtle yet critical piece in the Pacific puzzle. This boat's endurance in frigid, hostile waters reminds us that victory often hinged on such persistent, unglamorous patrols.

Ivan AI
Contributing Editor
Snakewater, Montana

Historical Context

Pacific War Timeline & Campaign Context

USS *S-32*'s patrols from August 1942 to May 1943 occurred during a critical phase of the Pacific War, coinciding with major campaigns such as the Guadalcanal Campaign (August 1942–February 1943) and the Aleutian Islands Campaign. The Aleutians, including Attu Island, were strategically significant as Japanese forces had occupied Attu and Kiska in June 1942, aiming to divert U.S. resources and secure northern flank positions. During *S-32*'s operations, the U.S. was intensifying efforts to isolate and recapture these islands, culminating in the Battle of Attu in May 1943. The patrol areas around Holtz Bay, Chichagof Harbor, and Sarana Bay were hotspots for Japanese resupply and reinforcement, with enemy defensive measures including destroyer patrols, reliance on poor weather for cover, and limited air surveillance due to harsh conditions.

Submarine Warfare Doctrine & Evolution

By 1942–1943, U.S. submarine doctrine emphasized commerce interdiction and reconnaissance to attrition Japanese shipping and support amphibious operations. Submarines like *S-32*, an older S-class boat, operated with technological limitations: unreliable torpedoes (evidenced by mixed results in attacks), early radar (SJ radar was invaluable but prone to defects), and communication challenges (e.g., radio frequency issues). Tactics involved submerged daylight patrols and night surface attacks, leveraging radar for navigation and targeting. *S-32*'s patrols reflected broader submarine force operations, focusing on attrition in peripheral theaters like the Aleutians. Innovations demonstrated included periscope photography for intelligence gathering, sound detection for tracking, and aggressive use of radar in low-visibility conditions, though mechanical failures highlighted the need for more reliable systems.

Strategic Significance of These Patrols

These patrols served key strategic objectives: commerce interdiction to disrupt Japanese logistics to Attu, reconnaissance to gather intelligence on enemy positions and hydrography, and attrition of naval assets. *S-32*'s actions, particularly in the Seventh War Patrol with successful attacks on a destroyer and submarine, contributed to degrading Japanese supply lines and supporting the U.S. offensive in the Aleutians. Notable successes included chart corrections that aided subsequent operations, while failures often stemmed from mechanical defects or weather hindrances. The patrols impacted enemy operations by forcing Japanese reliance on poor weather for resupply, delaying reinforcements, and providing critical data for the eventual recapture of Attu in May 1943.

Long-term Impact & Lessons Learned

S-32's experiences influenced post-war submarine evolution, underscoring the need for improved radar reliability, better torpedo performance, and enhanced crew habitability in extreme climates. Lessons learned, such as the importance of continuous radar search and robust electrical systems, informed designs of later submarines like the Gato and Balao classes. These patrols highlighted the value of stealth and electronic warfare, principles that remain relevant in modern submarine operations. *S-32*'s legacy lies in its contributions to the Aleutian Campaign, demonstrating the resilience of older boats and the critical role of submarines in theater isolation, paving the way for more integrated undersea warfare strategies in the Cold War era.

Glossary of Naval Terms

A

After Engine Room The rearmost of the two engine rooms on a fleet submarine, containing diesel engines for surface propulsion and battery charging.

After Torpedo Room The compartment at the stern of the submarine housing the stern torpedo tubes and torpedoes. Also referred to as the stern room.

B

Battle Stations An alert ordering all crew members to their assigned posts to prepare for combat.

Battle Surface A tactical maneuver where a submarine surfaces rapidly to engage a target with its deck gun(s).

Bends, The Decompression sickness, a painful and dangerous condition caused by ascending too quickly from deep water, which was a major risk for sailors escaping a sunken submarine.

Bow Tubes The torpedo tubes located in the bow (front) of the submarine. U.S. fleet submarines typically had six.

Bridge The open-air platform on top of the conning tower from which the submarine was commanded while on the surface.

Buoyancy The upward force exerted by a fluid that opposes the weight of an immersed object. Submarines control their buoyancy using ballast tanks to submerge and surface.

C

Circular Run A dangerous torpedo malfunction where the torpedo's guidance system fails, causing it to turn in a circle and potentially return to strike the submarine that fired it.

Conning Tower The small, pressure-tight compartment located above the main hull from which the submarine's periscopes were operated and attacks were directed while submerged.

D

Down the Throat (shot) A high-risk torpedo attack aimed directly at the bow of an oncoming enemy ship, requiring precise timing and positioning.

E

Electric Torpedo A type of torpedo, such as the Mark 18, propelled by electric motors and batteries. Its primary advantage was that it did not leave a visible wake of exhaust bubbles, making it harder for the enemy to detect and evade.

End Around A tactic where a submarine, using its superior surface speed, would run a wide course around an enemy convoy or warship, often at night, to position itself ahead for a submerged attack.

Escape Buoy A marker buoy that could be released from a sunken submarine to indicate its position to potential rescuers.

Escape Trunk A small, floodable compartment (airlock) used by the crew to exit a sunken submarine. Also known as an escape lock.

F

Fantail The rearmost, overhanging part of a ship's or submarine's stern deck.

Fish A common slang term for a torpedo.

Forward Torpedo Room The compartment at the bow of the submarine housing the forward torpedo tubes, torpedoes, and living quarters for some of the crew.

Frigate A type of warship, larger than a corvette but smaller than a destroyer, primarily used for escort and anti-submarine warfare duties.

Full Emergency Speed An order for the engines or motors to produce the maximum possible power for a short duration, used to evade an attack or escape a dangerous situation.

J

JANAC (Joint Army-Navy Assessment Committee) A U.S. committee established after World War II to officially analyze and verify combat claims, particularly ship sinkings, by U.S. forces.

K

Knot A unit of speed equal to one nautical mile per hour (approximately 1.15 mph or 1.85 km/h), used to measure the speed of ships and submarines.

L

Life Jacket A personal flotation device worn by crew members on the bridge or deck to prevent drowning if they were swept overboard.

M

Maneuvering Room The compartment in a submarine from which the electric motors and propulsion systems were controlled.

Mark 14 Torpedo The primary U.S. submarine torpedo at the start of World War II. It was a steam-powered weapon notorious for its early unreliability.

Mark 18 Torpedo A U.S. electric torpedo developed during World War II, reverse-engineered from a captured German torpedo. It was slower than the Mark 14 but was highly valued for being wakeless.

Momsen Lung A breathing device that allowed individual sailors to escape from a sunken submarine by recycling exhaled air through a chemical filter. Also known as an escape lung.

P

P-boat A colloquial term used by U.S. sailors for a Japanese patrol boat or submarine chaser, typically a small, lightly armed anti-submarine vessel.

Periscope An optical instrument with lenses and prisms that allows a submerged submarine to view the surface.

S

Stern Tubes The torpedo tubes located in the stern (rear) of the submarine. U.S. fleet submarines typically had four.

T

TDC (Torpedo Data Computer) A sophisticated analog computer that calculated the firing solution for a torpedo attack by integrating data on the target's course, speed, and range with the submarine's own data.

W

War Patrol An operational cruise by a submarine into enemy-controlled waters for the purpose of attacking enemy shipping and naval vessels.

Most Important Passages

Decision to Break Off Attack on Dutch Freighters

> *The decision of the Commanding Officer to break off the attack on the Dutch ore at anchor on October 17, on the grounds that he problem was not so difficult as not criticized. Since the difficult problem brought the commanding officers of a submarine frequently, and since there is evidence of Japanese shipping following thereon is in order, however. In recognition of this problem, and in accordance with instructions from higher authority, the Task Group Commander has directed attack upon all unidentifiable (p. 41)*

Significance: This passage reveals command decision-making under pressure and the tension between aggressive action and proper target identification. It shows the complexity of submarine warfare where commanders had to balance risk against rules of engagement, particularly regarding neutral vessels. The reference to higher authority instructions indicates this was a fleet-wide concern.

Depth Charge Attack and Torpedo Firing Sequence

> *Ensign JJV. Belladonna (Ensign Eye John) sighted degrees true range about 3700 yards. (Course 320 degrees) confirmed were: Lat 6°N, Long overcast with half moon behind clouds riding in visibility. Seas moderate rough from 200 degrees true. We went again forward with a deeper draft, probably a ship. Our position to HOLTZ BAY was 17 miles north of HOLTZ BAY. Went back to attack position and shifted to torpedo end and commenced night surface approach. The Jap submarine was apparently trying to be on a heading of 305 degrees true charging battery for there was no telltale exhaust on his surface for backing the starboard side. This exhaust smoke is what attracted me to him. I fired a first and then him to permit us to see his deck in our time and then only his conning tower. Assumed we were still undetected; closing range rapidly when at a range of 2500 yards he suddenly started smoking and I thought he was preparing to dive. It was shoot now or never for my torpedo were set at 4 feet. (p. 71)*

Significance: This passage captures a critical combat moment showing tactical decision-making during a night surface attack on a Japanese submarine. It demonstrates the commander's real-time assessment of enemy behavior, environmental conditions, and the split-second decision to fire torpedoes before losing the opportunity.

Torpedo Attack Results and Depth Charge Evasion

> *Fired 1 followed ten seconds later by 2. (Attack 2) The first torpedo fired short (in case of a miss seeking homerun) and the second fired at his conning tower. Went ahead full speed and changed course rapidly to the right and at 2100½ YOKE Dove. As*

we passed 50 feet in a very fast dive there was one (1) loud torpedo explosion. The number of high torpedoes were observed, when diving, heading true. The best time check gives 2 minutes and 20 seconds after firing the first torpedo until the torpedo explosion was heard by all hands. We dived immediately to avoid slow and tried to pick up his screws by sound. At no time previous or after torpedo explosion was sound able to hear propeller noises. We remained submerged for 100 feet attempting to pick up any identifiable sounds; none heard. (p. 71)

Significance: This passage documents the immediate aftermath of a torpedo attack, including the crew's evasion tactics and attempts to assess damage. It illustrates the uncertainty of submarine warfare where results were often unclear, and the need for rapid defensive maneuvering after an attack.

Major Radar Equipment Failure

On February 28 we experienced a wide trace and sometimes a double trace on screen. The following work was done: tightened many loose connections, fixed loose cap on fuse in control panel, and returned trace to screen. Found one condenser shorting out due to the plug protection cap of the cathode ray tube shorting condenser. Correcting this returned trace to normal shape. (Warning note: The range indication unit should be supported on 1/8" blocks when removed from case and worked on in an upright position because the indicator may slip down and protection cup extends beyond the bottom of chassis about 1/16".) Changed several tubes to range indicator as the press on screen was normal. The magnetron tube blower became very noisy but we decided to let it run removal as sea was next to impossible. The noise probably caused by bad bearings. On March 5 we got double trace on screen. This was caused by poor connection in the main terminal block of the receiver-transmitter unit. Worked on this and the trace were positive against the indicator under loads. These were positive against the indicator and insulation burned through in several places. These loads were then reserved and suspended clear of heater. Several days later it was found necessary to remove this heater (CSP 63128 P) because the heat was melting insulation. On March 16 the pulse and pipe bend to bounce too much. The magnetron tube appears black and may have lost its efficiency. Fours in use 450 so replaced with spare. Equipment now functions properly. The depth charge attack caused a large leak around packing of radar mast. A careful taking up on gland seemed to stop this leakage. (p. 81)

Significance: This passage details critical radar equipment failures and repairs, showing the technical challenges faced by submarine crews. The radar was essential for detecting enemy vessels and aircraft, and its malfunction severely compromised the submarine's effectiveness. The mention of depth charge damage also connects mechanical problems to combat stress on equipment.

Engine Room Flooding Emergency

Forced to slow to one engine to prevent flooding engine room for it is impossible to run on main induction only - the entire ship is under water at times, and the seas have shifted nearer the bow. At 1815 the seas started abating somewhat and we went ahead on both engines at 2/3 speed again. (p. 61)

Significance: This passage captures a dangerous moment when severe weather threatened to flood the engine room, forcing the commander to reduce speed. It illustrates the constant battle against the elements that submarines faced on the surface, and how environmental conditions could be as dangerous as enemy action.

Radio Communication Difficulties with Enemy Interference

On two occasions there was enemy interference on NPM's high frequency Fox schedules. No interference was noticed on their low frequency broadcasts. There was always a good, icularly on 4235 kcs. and 8470 kcs. Interference noted on all 4235 series and particularly on 4235 kcs. and 8470 kcs. All interference was many enemy stations containing Vs, dashes and garbled characters. Some stations, at times when the enemy would call our shore enemy would attempt to interfere immediately by holding his transmitter down or make long dashes. (p. 21)

Significance: This passage reveals Japanese attempts to jam or interfere with U.S. submarine communications, showing the electronic warfare dimension of submarine operations. Reliable communication with shore stations was critical for receiving orders and intelligence, making this interference a serious operational challenge.

Sound Conditions and Underwater Detection Challenges

In both areas patrolled it appeared that sound conditions were excellent. This was not true due to a mile or two of the shore line of any of the islands. The rush of the surf against the rocks could be heard for the WA, and would undoubtedly hamper good sound results. The temperature of the water was uniform to a degree Parenheit reduction from surface to a depth of 100 feet. This change appeared at 110 feet and then remained constant down to 180 feet. The average sea water temperature was 47 degrees F. The average of operations were conducted in water greater than 500 fathoms. The sound equipment appears to be ultra-sensitive in these areas. During submerged operations in KAYAN we heard explosions through the hull harbor about 35 miles distant. (p. 21)

Significance: This passage provides valuable technical intelligence about sonar conditions in the patrol area. Understanding sound propagation was critical for both detecting enemy vessels and avoiding detection. The ability to hear explosions 35 miles away demonstrates the excellent acoustic conditions but also the challenge of distinguishing relevant contacts.

Patrol Orders and Strategic Mission

Departed to patrol towards KISKA from a position north of SEMIDI ISLAND. At 1412 heard a series of loud under water explosions. Patrolled to within 12 miles

> *KISKA; patrolled north of KISKA 10 1/2 miles KISKA; patrolled northeast observer-type morning, surfaced 2015 just south-east of KISKA 10 1/2 miles KISKA and charted batteries. Visibility excellent. (p. 31)*

Significance: This passage establishes the strategic context of the patrol, showing operations near Japanese-held Kiska in the Aleutian Islands. The patrol's proximity to enemy-held territory and the mention of underwater explosions indicates active combat operations in the area, highlighting the strategic importance of the Aleutians campaign.

Air Compressor Failure During Critical Operations

> *At 0445 (Y) 12 April the water jacket pump for starboard CBR air compressor registered excessive pressure and jammed. The compressor was immediately secured. The first stage cooler coils were removed and tested under 100 pounds pressure. A split, about four inches long, was discovered (p. 101)*

Significance: This passage documents a critical mechanical failure of the air compressor, which was essential for operating torpedoes, blowing ballast tanks, and other vital submarine functions. The timing during active patrol operations made this particularly serious, demonstrating the constant maintenance challenges faced by submarine crews.

Investigation of Submarine Sighting at Attu Cove

> *Surfaced and closed at a standard speed both engines. Fog again. Submerged in full gale and headed towards HOLTZ to investigate for submarine sighted in ATTU COVE by Army sighting plane of yesterday at 0730 (Y). The charts so named on charts but we are assuming this cove gave negative information. Periscope depth control is practically impossible without breaching. Fog lifted - sighted land bearing 096, 232, 265, 310 gyro took a rough azimuth and found a 54° westerly error in gyro. Bearings compare at this time is using very erratic. Information obtained from corrected bearings showed us to be about seven miles north of ONEKOTAN TO ISLAND and on western side of ONEKOTAN TO ISLAND. By back tracking position, found that we had passed through four miles south of PARAUSHIRU. Steered by wind and sea while repairs were effected to gyro compass. Fog again closed in. Radar still out of commission. (p. 111)*

Significance: This passage illustrates the challenges of navigation in poor weather with equipment failures (radar and gyro compass out), while attempting to investigate a reported enemy submarine. It shows how multiple system failures compounded operational difficulties and the crew's resourcefulness in using alternative navigation methods.

War Patrol Reports

S-32 (SS-137)

WWII PATROL FILE

ALL MATERIAL ON THIS REEL IS DECLASSIFIED

J.A. KOONTZ

S–32

(SS–137: dp. 854 (surf.), 1,062 (subm.); l. 219'3"; b. 20'8"; dr. 15'11" (mean); s. 14.5 k. (surf.), 11 k. (subm.); cpl. 42; a. 1 4", 4 21" tt.; cl. *S–1*)

S–32 (SS–137) was laid down on 12 April 1918 by the Union Iron Works, San Francisco, Calif.; launched on 11 January 1919; sponsored by Miss Margaret Tynan; and commissioned on 15 June 1922, Lt. Edward E. Hazlett, Jr., in command.

Soon after commissioning, *S–32*, assigned to Submarine Division 17 and homeported at San Pedro, Calif., was ordered to New London, Conn. She was decommissioned there on 25 September 1922 and after engineering alterations by the prime contractor, the Electric Boat Co., and the engineering sub-contractor, the New London Ship and Engine Co., she was recommissioned on 21 February 1923. Temporary duty with Division 11 then took her south to the Caribbean and the Canal Zone for winter exercises with the Fleet, after which she rejoined the S-boats of her division, now designated Division 16, and returned to San Pedro.

During the summer of 1923, she participated in cold weather exercises in the Aleutians. In the fall, she resumed local operations off southern California and, that winter, she returned to the Canal Zone. In April 1924, she moved back to San Pedro, whence she operated into 1925. Early that year, however, her division was transferred to the Asiatic Fleet and its submarines shifted to Mare Island to prepare for the transpacific crossing.

On 15 April 1925, *S–32* departed San Francisco for the Philippines. She arrived at Cavite in mid-summer and through the winter of 1926 conducted local exercises in the Luzon area. That spring, she deployed to the China coast, conducting exercises both en route to and from her summer base, the former German base at Tsingtao. Overhaul followed her September return to the Philippines and completed an annual employment schedule which she maintained for the next six years.

In 1932, Division 16 was ordered back to the eastern Pacific. *S–32* departed Manila Bay on 2 May and, at the end of the month, arrived at Pearl Harbor, her homeport for the next five years. In June 1937, she sailed for the east coast. In August, she reported for inactivation at Philadelphia and, on 7 December, she was decommissioned and berthed at League Island.

Within two years, however, Europe was at war. Hostilities soon extended across the Atlantic; and, in the summer of 1940, *S–32* began activation.

Recommissioned on 18 September 1940 and assigned to Division 52, *S–32* conducted trials out of New London through November and, in December, proceeded to the Panama Canal Zone, whence she operated until April 1941. She then returned to New London but, toward the end of April, moved south again, to Bermuda. Through May, she patrolled and conducted training exercises out of the St. George's base acquired in the destroyers for bases agreement. In late June, she resumed exercises out of New London. In September, she moved down to Philadelphia for an overhaul; and, by December, she was back in Connecticut. With 1942, however, she received orders back to Panama.

She arrived at Coco Solo in February. During the spring, she conducted two defensive patrols in the Pacific approaches to the canal and, in June, she proceeded to San Diego en route to the Aleutians. In early July, she arrived at Dutch Harbor; and, on the 7th, she departed that Unalaska base on her first offensive war patrol. She patrolled the fog-covered waters of Rat Island and Oglala passes into August; then shifted to an area north of Attu, returning to Dutch Harbor on the 10th.

Twelve days later, she departed on her fourth war patrol. Moving westward, she hunted in the Japanese traffic lanes between Kiska and Attu during the first week of the patrol. On the 28th, leaks developed in the after trim tank, but were compensated for by placing nine tons of water in the forward trim tanks. Although this meant that space was left to accommodate water for only one torpedo reload, depth control was regained, and, with fuel suction shifted forward, reload capability slowly improved. On 29 August, she was off Amchitka to check for enemy shipping in sheltered areas on that island's north coast; then, on the 31st, she headed east to cover the Allied occupation of Adak. On 14 September, she returned to the junction of Rat Island and Oglala passes where she continued her patrol for another six days. On the 20th, she headed for Dutch Harbor.

Arriving on the 23rd, *S-32* departed again on 8 October. During a trim dive, a fuel discrepancy, caused by the presence of water in the line during fueling at Dutch Harbor, was discovered. On the 12th, the S-boat ran out of reserve fuel in the No. 3 main ballast tank. The discrepancy was approximately 9,000 gallons, but *S-32* continued west, into the Kurils.

On the 17th, she arrived off Paramushiro and, that evening, she took up station off the southeast coast of the island to patrol the entrances to Musashi Wan and Onekotan Strait. On the morning of the 18th, she sighted two ships at anchor in Musashi Wan; and, after a periscope check disclosed no other ships in the area, she began working her way to an attack position west or southwest of the targets. Moving slowly, with short and infrequent periscope exposures, through the calm and poorly charted bay, she went up for a final check at 1023. While looking, she struck an uncharted sand bar. The S-boat, her tubes ready for firing, angled up 10°. Her depth gauge showed 32 feet. During the next few seconds she slid over the bar, apparently showing periscope shears, bow, and, possibly, the whole bridge structure; then, over the bar, she took a down angle at high speed. At 1025, she fired. Two torpedoes, set at six feet, were sent against each of the targets. On firing the fourth and final "fish", she changed course and maneuvered at high speed toward the open sea. Two explosions were heard as she cleared the immediate area. At 1045, she came to periscope depth to observe the damage.

One of the targets was afire amidships and had settled somewhat; she was anchored in shallow water and might have been resting on the bottom. The second target was obscured by the first. *S-32* went to 80 feet and proceeded out of the bay. At 1205, she resumed her patrol east out of Onekotan Strait. That evening, she turned toward the Aleutians; and, on the 27th, she arrived at Dutch Harbor.

From Dutch Harbor, *S-32* returned to San Diego. Overhaul followed her 11 November arrival; and, from 21 to 25 December, she tested newly installed equipment: a fathometer, radar, and keel-mounted sound gear. From 28 December 1942 to 26 January 1943, she provided services to the West Coast Sound School; and, on 6 February, she headed north toward Dutch Harbor.

S-32 departed Unalaska on her 6th war patrol on 2[illegible] February. En route to her assigned station off Attu, she encountered very rough seas, strong winds, rain, mist, and fog. On the 26th, rolling was measured as much as 65° to starboard.

Progress west was slow; but, on 1 March, she set a course toward Holtz Bay to check for enemy shipping. The next day, heavy mist and fog hindered her reconnaisance of Stellar Cove; and she turned to the coastal shipping lanes to intercept enemy traffic between Cape Wrangell and Holtz Bay. The entrances to the latter, to Chichagof Harbor, and to Sarana Bay, however, were her primary hunting grounds. On the night of 9 March, off Holtz Bay, she attacked and damaged an enemy destroyer, then underwent a brief depth charging. Leaks caused by the depth charging were minimized, and *S-32* continued her patrol.

Four nights later, on the 13th, seventeen miles north of Holtz Bay, she attacked an enemy submarine which was lying to on the surface with her engines smoking. At 2059, the S-boat fired two torpedoes at ten-second intervals at the enemy. At 2100, she went deep; and, as she passed 50 feet, one torpedo exploded. At 2120, *S-32* came to periscope depth, but the fog had closed in. The target was no longer visible.

On the afternoon of the 15th, a second submarine was sighted. The weather, for the first time, was "perfect for a periscope approach." At 1727, *S-32* fired a three-torpedo spread; estimated range 2,500 yards; track angle favorable. About two and a half minutes later, a muffled explosion was heard in the torpedo room. No explosion was heard by the control party. The S-boat went to periscope depth. Smoke was pouring skyward from the enemy's conning tower. A photograph was taken of the scene as the damaged target headed for the nearest beach. At 1736, however, the enemy disappeared from view. Sound reported that the enemy's screws had stopped.

S-32 departed the Attu area early on the morning of the 17th. On the 20th, she moored at Dutch Harbor; and, nine days later, she again sailed west. En route to Attu, cold weather caused icing on the superstructure, but the seas remained fairly calm and the sun was occasionally visible. On 3 March, however, as she approached Attu, more normal Aleutian weather closed in. From then to the 16th, snow and rain storms were almost continuous; seas were rough; winds were strong; and periods of sunlight were limited. At 0157 on the 10th, while patrolling on a north-south line out of Holtz Bay, *S-32* picked up a target on radar, some 7,000 yards away. Ten minutes later, a second smaller ship was detected ahead of the first target. Five minutes after the appearance of the second ship on the screen, the first ship was sighted, range about 2,000 yards. *S-32* fired four torpedoes. Two very loud explosions were heard and were followed by distant rumblings. At 0219, at a range of just over 3,500 yards, all traces of the ships disappeared from the screen.

On 16 March, *S-32* set a course for Dutch Harbor. On the 20th, she arrived and commenced refit. On 4 May, she again sailed west. En route to the Kurils, she patrolled across possible Japanese reinforcement routes to Kiska and Attu, but almost zero visibility during the passage hindered hunting. On the 12th, she entered her assigned area off Paramushiro. The next day, she obtained her first fix, off Onekotan, and commenced patrolling across the approaches to Onekotan Strait and Musashi Wan. Visibility remained poor; seas were rough. Her radar, which had gone out of commission on the 11th, functioned improperly throughout her short time on station. On the 15th, the port main motor armature developed a zero resistance to ground. Repeated repair attempts failed, and the motor was secured. *S-32* turned back toward Unalaska and moored at Dutch Harbor on the 23rd.

On the 27th, the submarine departed the Aleutians for the last time; and, on 6 June, she arrived at San

Diego, where she provided training services for the remainder of World War II. Then designated for inactivation, she arrived at San Francisco on 13 September 1945 and was decommissioned at Mare Island on 19 October. Her name was struck from the Navy list on 1 November 1945, and her hulk was sold for scrapping to the Learner Co., Oakland, Calif., in May 1946.

S-32 earned five battle stars during World War II.

Dictionary of

American Naval Fighting Ships

VOLUME VI

Historical Sketches—Letters R through S

Appendices—Submarine Chasers (SC)
Eagle-Class Patrol Craft (PE)

WITH A FOREWORD BY

ADMIRAL JAMES L. HOLLOWAY III, United States Navy,
THE CHIEF OF NAVAL OPERATIONS

AND AN INTRODUCTION BY

VICE ADMIRAL EDWIN B. HOOPER, United States Navy, Retired,
THE DIRECTOR OF NAVAL HISTORY

NAVAL HISTORY DIVISION
DEPARTMENT OF THE NAVY
WASHINGTON: 1976

U. S. S. S-32
SUBMARINE DIVISION 44

SUBMARINE SQUADRON TWENTY

DECLASSIFIED.

AUG 24 1941 4 27 PM

[illegible]

[illegible]
Serial [illegible]

U. S. S. S-32
SUBMARINE DIVISION 44

CONFIDENTIAL

Subject: [illegible] patrol conducted during period [illegible] August, 1941.

- -

[illegible]: "[illegible]" [illegible] to be satisfactory but the present ration allowance precludes its use.

FROZEN MEATS: Frozen meat has been used by this ship for the last two weeks. It is excellent and 30 days fresh meat can be stored in the allotted space in the present ice box with ease. Ration cost is increased.

NIGHT LOOKOUTS: Watch standing was in accordance with existing instructions and proved satisfactory. A total of 18 men for a war patrol is essential.

SMOKING: No restrictions were placed on smoking during the all day submerged patrol. There was no discomfort as a result of this smoking and I believe there was less smoking than would have been the case if the old system of lighting the smoking lamp for 15 minutes every hour had been used.

7. The following recommendations are made:

SANITARY TANKS: Install a sanitary tank in the engine room to take care of the officers head and the galley sink. Install a sanitary tank in the control room [illegible] to take care of the crews head. Alternative - provide suitable chemical heads.

#1 →

TOILET BOWLS: Expedite installation of [illegible] toilet bowls. A [illegible] fire [illegible] would probably shatter present bowls.

#2 →

MAGNETIC COMPASS [illegible]: Change magnetic compass [illegible] to prevent fogging when submerged for long periods in cold water.

[illegible]: Install moisture traps in ventilation system to [illegible] as "[illegible]". [illegible] this ship looked like it has been in a hard rain storm after being submerged at 120 feet in 45° F. water for a period of four hours. Bedding was kept dry by covering bunks with oil cloth.

#3 →

OPERATION ORDER: It is recommended that the next patrol operation order be more specific regarding diving while proceeding to and from assigned area.

[signature]
[illegible] DUKE.

[initials]

U. S. S. S-32
SUBMARINE DIVISION 44

CONFIDENTIAL

NARRATIVE

MONDAY, AUGUST 18, 1941:

Underway from alongside U.S.S. [illegible] in Provincetown Harbor, at 0500 in accordance with Comsubron-[illegible] serial 0153. Proceeded to patrol area #5, arriving at 0900. At 1011 sighted two observation planes on horizon to Southward. Made quick dive to 60 feet and then returned to periscope depth, at which time three planes and a battleship were visible bearing 180°, distance 10 miles. Closed on course 180° to attack. [illegible] screened by two [illegible] planes were seen to be searching well ahead. When range [illegible] at 10,000 yards increased depth to 100 feet and continued attack by sound. At 1050 fired four water slugs. [illegible] remained [illegible] until 1210, at which time surfaced and continued surface patrol.

TUESDAY, AUGUST 19, 1941:

[illegible] patrol [illegible] area #5 on course [illegible] [illegible] small fishing craft. [illegible] to 100 feet at 0800. [illegible] stop trim and listening watch throughout [illegible]. Came up to periscope depth at noon to send position report. [illegible] with [illegible]. All other [illegible]. Increased depth to 100 feet. [illegible] stop trim and listening watch until 1800 at which time surfaced. [illegible] from Northwest, [illegible] with 1000 yards visibility. Stood in toward Cape Ann [illegible]. [illegible] obtained [illegible] bearings and found [illegible] 3.5 miles to the South during the day. Patrolled [illegible] Eastern section of area [illegible].

WEDNESDAY, AUGUST 20, 1941:

Patrolled Western section of area until daylight - heavy fog; sounding for [illegible]. At daylight stood in toward Cape Ann to fix position. At [illegible] sighted Cape Ann, visibility increased to 6000 yards. 0900 sighted plane to South, position angle 00°. This plane could be heard before it was sighted. As visibility had increased to 6000 yards [illegible] 100 feet to avoid detection. [illegible] At 1100 came to periscope depth to fix position and sighted Navy Blimp four miles to Westward, elevation about 500 feet. Blimp searched Western section of area for about 10 minutes and then headed away on Southerly course. Increased depth to 100 feet, maintaining stop trim and listening watch until noon. Came to periscope depth and sent out position report. Returned to 100 feet and maintained stop trim until 1400 when decreased depth to [illegible] feet to maintain periscope watch and attempt to get a stop trim at periscope depth. One-half hour longest stop trim obtained at periscope depth, but two new officers were being trained as diving officers. Surfaced at 1900 and started night surface patrol. Numerous ships sighted but no darkened targets.

ENCLOSURE (A)

CONFIDENTIAL

U. S. S. S-32
SUBMARINE DIVISION 44

WAR DIARY (CONT'D)

THURSDAY, AUGUST 21, 1941:

Patrolled entire area during night. No target sighted. At 0800 submerged to periscope depth. 0830 increased depth to 100 feet, maintaining stop trim and listening watch. Numerous fishing boats overhead. At 0930 returned to periscope depth. Considerable trouble was experienced with both periscopes fogging badly after being exposed to the air for a few minutes. This continued throughout the day. After a periscope started to fog the only way found to clear it was to lower for at least ten minutes. The fog formed on the inside of the periscope. No targets sighted during submerged patrol. Surfaced at 1900 and started of[?] surface patrol on East and West courses from Cape Ann Light.

FRIDAY, AUGUST 22, 1941:

Surface patrol as before, on East and West courses from Cape Ann Light. At 1215, while on course 090° true sighted CA coming out of haze on bearing 115° true - made quick dive. Cruiser believed to be Vincennes, on course 090° true, speed 17 knots, range 10,000 yards - attack impossible. At 1300 Cruiser disappeared in haze. At 1320 surfaced and proceeded on both engines to re-establish contact. At 1400 reached limit of area and resumed surface patrol on East and West course, at one engine speed. At 2000 started patrolling on a North and South line from a point three miles to the East of Cape Ann. No targets sighted.

SATURDAY, AUGUST 23, 1941:

Patrolling on a North and South line from a point 3 miles to the East of Cape Ann Light. No targets sighted during darkness. At 0700 took departure of Cape Ann and set course for Race Point, proceeding to Provincetown Harbor. At 1013 sighted 3 observation planes just under the sun, distance 8 miles, visibility on surface 4000 yards. Made quick dive and changed direction. 1030 surfaced and proceeded on both engines. At 1048 sighted PBY coming out of sun headed for me, distance 1.5 miles. Made quick dive. 1057 surfaced and proceeded toward Provincetown. 1300 anchored in Provincetown Harbor.

ENCLOSURE (A)

CONFIDENTIAL

U. S. S. S-32
SUBMARINE DIVISION 44 52

DATA OBTAINED

(a). Daily expenditure of potable water in gallons per man per day.

Sunday Aug.17th	Tuesday Aug.19th	Wednesday Aug.20th	Thursday Aug.21st	Friday Aug.22	Saturday Aug.23rd.
1.8	2.3	2.2	2.2	2.2	2.4

For six days, average gallons per man per day .... [illegible].3

(b). Average daily expenditure of battery water .... 18 gal.

(c). Daily expenditure of provisions:

(On next page)

ENCLOSURE (B)

U. S. S. S-32
SUBMARINE DIVISION 44

CONFIDENTIAL

DATA DETAILED (CONT'D)

MONDAY			TUESDAY			WEDNESDAY		
Bread, wheat	16	Lbs	Crackers	2	Lbs	Crackers	2	Lbs
Flour "	10	"	Bread, wheat	15	"	Bread, wheat	15	"
Luncheon meat	2	"	Flour, wheat	10	"	Flour "	10	"
Sausage, Vienna, Tn	2	"	Lunch. meat	2	"	Beef, [illegible]	[illegible]	"
Bacon	[illegible]	"	Hams, sp. Tn.	[illegible]	"	Luncheon meat	2	"
Sausage, Frank	[illegible]	"	Beef, roast	6	"	Bacon	[illegible]	"
Beef, [illegible] roast	[illegible]	"	Chicken, roast	40	"	Hams, sp	[illegible]	"
Beans, Lima, Frozen	10	"	Pork loin	[illegible]	"	Beef, roast	[illegible]	"
Beans, stg. Tn.	[illegible]	"	Peas, Tn	[illegible]	"	Beans, dry	[illegible]	"
Cabbage, Fresh	4	"	Tomatoes, Tn	[illegible]	"	Celery, Fresh	1	"
Celery "	1	"	Cabbage, fresh	2	"	Onions, "	2	"
Lettuce "	2	"	Carrots "	1	"	Potatoes "	[illegible]	"
Onions "	5	"	Celery "	1	"	Peaches, Tn	[illegible]	"
Peppers "	[illegible]	"	Lettuce "	2	"	Pineapple, Tn	4	"
Potatoes "	35	"	Onions "	4	"	Jam	[illegible]	"
Tomatoes "	[illegible]	"	Peppers "	1	"	Apples, fresh	10	"
Cucumbers "	4	"	Potatoes "	30	"	Cocoa	[illegible]	"
Jam	2	"	Apples, Tn	[illegible]	"	Coffee	10	"
Apples "	[illegible]	"	Pineapple, Tn	2	"	Tea	1	"
Cocoa	[illegible]	"	Jam	12	"	Milk, dry	2	"
Coffee	[illegible]	"	Apples, fresh	10	"	Milk, evap	18	"
Milk, evap	18	"	Cocoa	3	"	Butter	7	"
Butter	7	"	Coffee	12	"	[illegible]	10	[illegible]
Cereals, prep	12	Pks.	Tea	1	"	Cheese	3	Lbs
Cheese	3	Lbs	Milk, dry	2	"	[illegible]	[illegible]	Doz
Lard	1	"	Milk, evap	12	"	[illegible]	1	Lb
Vinegar	1	gal	Butter	7	"	Sugar, gran	15	[illegible]
Sugar, gran	15	Lbs	Cereals, prep	10	Pks	Pickles	2	"
Sugar, powdered	2	Lbs	Oats, rolled	1	"	Salt	2	"
Salt	2	"	Cheese, Swiss	3	Lbs	[illegible]	1	gal
Tomato juice	1	gal.	Eggs	10	Doz	Jello (assorted)	2	Pks
			Lard	5	Lbs	Tomato juice	2	gal
			Catsup	1	gal	Coffee, [illegible]	10	Oz
			Oil, salad	1	"			
			Vinegar	[illegible]	"			
			Sugar, gran	15	Lbs			
			Pickles	3	"			
			Salt	2	"			
			Tomato juice	1	gal			
			Corn beef hash	7	Lbs.			
Cost of ration	25.56			[illegible]			[illegible]	
	(20.5432)			([illegible])			([illegible])	

-2-

U. S. S. S-32
SUBMARINE DIVISION 44

Average daily cost of ration for six days

-3-

CONFIDENTIAL

U. S. S. S-32
SUBMARINE DIVISION 44

DATA OBTAINED (CONT'D)

(e). Amount of potable water distilled daily (gallons) 0000 to 2400.

Monday Aug. 18th	Tuesday Aug. 19th	Wednesday Aug. 20th	Thursday Aug. 21st	Friday Aug. 22nd	Saturday Aug. 23rd
106	54	100	104	178	0

(f). Fuel used daily (gallons) 0000 to 2400.

Monday	Tuesday	Wednesday	Thursday	Friday	Saturday
320	270	382	410	495	385

(f). KW discharged during submerged patrols, including auxiliary load;

Tuesday	Wednesday	Thursday
406.7	602.1	628.5

(2) KW auxiliary load on surface average (hourly) 25.0

(3) KW charged daily (0000 to 2400):

Monday	Tuesday	Wednesday	Thursday	Friday	Saturday
0	407	2204	2095	[illegible]	0

(g). TEMPERATURES:

	Mon	Tue	Wed	Thur	Fri	Sat
High	78	75	77	77	78	77
Low	73	73	75	75	75	74
Relative humidity	80%	79%	80%	79%	80%	70

(h). Hours of continuous balancing with stop trim guide:

Monday	Tuesday	Wednesday	Thursday	Friday	Saturday
Not attempted	6 hrs 25 min.	3 hrs 30 min.	4 hrs 13 min.	Not Attempted	Not attempted

(i). Time taken on emergency quick dives:

Dive No.	Reason for dive	Time from enemy sighted to sound diving alarm	Time from diving alarm to periscope depth	Total time to periscope depth from enemy sighted
1	Planes	15 sec.	60 Sec.	84 Sec.
2	Plane	10 "	65 "	75 "
3	Cruiser	15 "	65 "	80 "
4	3 planes	10 "	60 "	70 "
5	Plane	15 "	65 "	80 "

-4-

CONFIDENTIAL (B)

S-32's FIRST OFFENSIVE WAR PATROL IS NUMBERED "THIRD". THERE ARE NO PATROLS MISSING FROM THIS COLLECTION.

1st copy

DECLASSIFIED

CONFIDENTIAL

U.S.S. S-32 - REPORT OF THIRD WAR PATROL.

PERIOD FROM: July 7, 1942 to August 10, 1942.

AREAS: RAT[illegible] and ATTU THREE

OPERATION ORDER: Commander Task Group 8.5 Operation Order No. 4-42, and changes there to in accordance Commander Task Group 8.5 despatches 090050, 090141 of July, 1942 and 020306 of August 1942.

1. NARRATIVE:

In accordance with Commander Task Group Eight Point Five Operation Order No. 4-42 and changes there to the following report of the Third War Patrol of the U.S.S. S-32 is submitted.

Zone WILLIAM used for all times.

All patrolling by this vessel was carried out submerged during daylight, except in area ATTU THREE. At night we had to lie to from three to four hours using both engines on battery charge. After that time we patrolled remainder of night on one engine while finishing the battery charge on the other. During submerged patrol periscope depth was maintained and observations varied from continuous to not greater than five to ten minute intervals depending upon weather conditions. Length of daily submerged operations varied from 16 to 17.5 hours.

1200 W. 7/7/42

Departed DUTCH HARBOR for area ADAK SOUTH at 1200 William, July 7, 1942 via AKUTAN PASS.

At 1434, while in AKUTAN PASS sighted medium-grey painted periscope of submarine broad on the starboard bow range estimated at 1500 yards. Imediately changed course towards periscope at full speed. Periscope disappeared but not until an estimate of submarines course had been made (300 degrees true). After periscope failed to reappear in next four minutes course was changed radically to the left and zig-zag procedure was carried out proceeding through the remainder of the pass. A contact message was sent to task group commander but great difficulty in clearing same was experienced due to communication conditions in this area. The despatch was finally cleared through radio BREMERTON.

At 2300 the scheduled radio tests with Radio DUTCH HARBOR were a failure.

Filmed 87851

ENCLOSURE (C)

CONFIDENTIAL

U.S.S. S-32 - REPORT OF THIRD WAR PATROL.

- -

7/8/42 At 0100, 0130 and 0235 sighted glow of light bearing 320, 325 and 350 degrees true, respectively. From plot assumed source of glow to be from volcano.

At 0530 sighted Navy PBY plane bearing 030 degrees true on easterly course, distance 6 miles. No exchange of recognition signals made. Undetected.

At 1600 received orders to proceed to a new area (RATAN).

7/9/42 to 7/10/42 Enroute to patrol area; arrived in area at 1000, July 10, 1942. Commenced submerged patrol during daylight hours. Heavy fog at least 90 percent of the time. Seas **Moderate** Current Varying.

7/11/42 Patrolled OGLALA PASS. Discovered varying currents of from 1 to 4 knots in force and varying directions. Light density layers occurred as proved by sudden loss of depth from periscope depth to 75 feet in 2 to 3 seconds. This area would be a tricky spot for any periscope approach. Examined North east shore line AMCHITKA ISLAND - results negative.

1/42 to /13/42 Patrolled area and investigated shores and bays of RAT ISLAND, and LITTLE SITKIN. Took careful search of GUNNER'S COVE. Results negative.

/14/42 to /18/42 Patrolled in area. Examined shore line and bays of SEMISOPOCHNOI, AMCHITKA AND RAT ISLANDS; especially CONSTANTINE HARBOR, KIROLOF BAY and GUNNER'S COVE. Results negative. Between 1635 and 1855 William on 14 July heard many explosions. Believed to be bombing attacks on KISKA. Received Commander Task Group 8.5 briefed operation order No. 6-42.

1250 W /19/42 Received Commander Task Group 8.5 special order for July 22, 1942. Acknowledged receipt by encoded despatch.

/20/42 /21/42 Patrolled in area. No land sighted for 56 hours. Foggy.

/22/42 Conducted patrol in assigned section of area. Maintained a position that would enable us to guard tracks of any vessels attempting to navigate RAT ISLANDS PASS, OGLALA PASS and the pass to eastward of LITTLE SITKIN ISLAND.

/23/42 /24/42 Continued patrol in especially designated sector of area. Continuous fog and varying currents made accomplishment of Mission a matter guess work and luck.

CONFIDENTIAL

U.S.S. S-32 - REPORT OF THIRD WAR PATROL.

- -

25/42
/26/42 Orders for restricted operations cancelled until 27 July. Continued patrol throughout entire area and passes. Results negative. At 0617, while attempting to make a land fall to fix position, sighted an object in the water resembling a buoy shaped like an aerial bomb, painted red. This object was tear drop in shape with tail fins and a body fin around large end set at an angle to longitudinal axis. There was a white diamond shaped float attached by a two fathom line. No one on board could identify the object, and one man believed it to be a type of aerial mine. In order to make certain we circled the object at several hundred yards distance and sank it by rifle fire. We then believed that it was just a buoy of some sort.

923 W
/25/42 Sound reported propeller noise bearing 030 degrees true. Periscope examinations negative. Sound contact not too positive.

/27/42 Resumed patrol in special sector of area. Heavy fog all day. At 1006 William sound reported a propeller noise on bearing 050 degrees true. Changed course to bearing and maintained contact intermittently for thirty minutes. At one time sound reported a propeller count of 90 rpms. At no time was sound contact very loud and it was believed vessel to be at least six miles away since sound conditions appeared excellent in this area away from land. There were so many strange noises in this area that unless the sound contacts were more positive than the foregoing no definite contacts were assumed. At times our own propeller beat was heard all around the dial even at slowest speed on one motor. At all times visibility through the periscope was maximum and results were negative. We were about to surface and try a look from the bridge when the fog settled in suddenly and prevented such procedure. At 2239 William heard distant explosion. Surfaced after dark.

/28/42 Conducted patrol in special sector of area. Navigated by dead reckoning past two days with no signs of change in persistent foggy weather. At 0530 William July 29, 1942 sighted LITTLE SITKIN ISLAND through a momentary break in the fog and obtained fix. At 1435 William heard a series of explosions; and again at 1516. Assumed to be bombing of KISKA. Periscope observations negative.

/30/42
/31/42 Continued patrol in special sector of area. At 0150 William, 31 July, received despatch from task force commander deferring operations accordance latest plan.

ENCLOSURE (C)

Expected change in area assignment, but none was received. Between 1436 and 2231 William 31 July, heard many explosions and assumed them to be a result of bombing of KISKA.

8/1/42 Since no orders to change area were received, patrolling was continued in special sector during the forenoon and then I decided to leave that sector and patrol the entire area as before; especially shore line and coves. I had missed one serial despatch and assumed this was the change in special orders. Between 1812 and 1820 heard several explosions. Visibility away from land was very good today.

8/2/42 At 0207 received orders to proceed to and patrol new area north of ATTU. These orders changed me from an area we were not in to the new area. I then realized the missing despatch would clarify every thing. Before we could get a message off requesting a repetition of missing despatch, it was repeated on the Fox schedule. We had been ordered to return to DUTCH HARBOR, then changed to proceed to and patrol area ADAK NORTH Prior latest orders to new area north of ATTU. We got under way and proceeded north from AMCHITKA PASS to a point on the track prescribed in our orders and proceeded to new patrol area. We sent a despatch notifying group commander of our actions.

8/3/42 At 2042 entered newly assigned patrol area and commenced conducting patrol on surface during times of good visibility. Have order to send weather reports at 0200 and 1400 William daily.

8/4/42 to 8/6/42 Continued patrol in this area, remaining on surface as much as possible. Submerged only during very poor visibility conditions. Received order to transmit any marked change in weather after first report required on 7 August.

8/7/42 Made weather reports to task group commander at 0247, 0518 and 1501 (all times William).

8/8/42 to 8/11/42 Received orders to leave patrol area and return Dutch Harbor.

Enroute from area to base. Bombardment of KISKA by our main body accomplished August 8, 1942.

At 0615 August 10, 1942 sighted Army medium bomber type B26 and dove immediately. Surfaced at 0640 and continued course and speed.

Arrived 2230 William DUTCH HARBOR 10 August, 1942.

CONFIDENTIAL

U.S.S. S-32 - REPORT OF THIRD WAR PATROL.

2. WEATHER.

(a) Enroute patrol area RATAN - foggy, moderate to heavy seas - wind and seas from Southwest.

(b) Area RATAN. Fog covered entire area to such an extent that land was obscured 85 percent of the period on station. There were nine days during which no land was sighted. Average visibility was about one mile. Afternoons generally, were much clearer than mornings. Land fog seemed always present. Aside from the fog the weather was good, very little rain, moderate winds and seas. Average air temperature was 48 degrees F.

(c) Enroute area ATTU THREE, it was foggy. In the area fog persisted 50 percent of the time. Seas and winds moderate. Average visibility three miles.

(d) Enroute area to DUTCH HARBOR occassional fog banks. Seas and winds moderate.

3. TIDAL DATA.

(a) Enroute area RATAN currents were negligible.

(b) Area RATAN. In RAT ISLAND AND OGLALA PASSES currents followed the contours of these passes and force varied from 0.5 to 4.0 knots. Between LITTLE SITKIN, AMCHITKA, AND SEMISOPOCHNOI the overall current for any twenty-four hour period was: set 075 to 125 degrees true and drift from 0.2 to 0.4. The unpredictable currents and varying density layers in RAT ISLAND and OGLALA PASSES made depth control extremely difficult.

(c) Area RATAN to area ATTU THREE the current was negligible.

(d) Area ATTU THREE. The observations in this area proved overall set 080 degrees true and drift 0.4 to 1.3 knots.

(e) Enroute DUTCH HARBOR. Current appeared to set 080 degrees with drift 1 knot.

4. NAVIGATIONAL AIDS.

Area RATAN. Mountains and tangents on LITTLE SITKIN and SEMISOPOCHNOI gave good fixes when within ten miles of either island. Poor fixes resulted when points from these two islands were used together. It is believed that SEMISOPOCHNOI is two miles to the north of its charted position. Fixes on AMCHITKA and RAT ISLAND were inaccurate. The islands are low and all tangents look alike when partly covered with fog. There are many small peaks on these two islands that would make good land marks if they were on the chart. No opportunity

ENCLOSURE (C)

CONFIDENTIAL

U.S.S. S-32 - REPORT OF THIRD WAR PATROL.

- -

was had to establish these peaks accurately on the chart. Navigation is largely a matter of guesswork around these two islands. Extreme caution is necessary. It is believed that AYUGADAK POINT on RAT ISLAND extends one-half mile farther East than is shown on the chart. Pictures of these islands showing names of peaks and tangents would be a great help to navigation in this area. The chart referred to H.O. #5640 (Confidential).

5. None sighted.

6. AIRCRAFT SIGHTED.

DATE	TIME	TYPE	POSITION	COURSE	ALTITUDE
8 July	0530	PBY	Lat. 52-52 N. Long. 168-46 W.	070	2000 ft.
10 August	0616	B26	Lat. 53-57 N. Long. 171-20 W.	250	1500 ft.

7. No attacks made.

8. None experienced.

9. MAJOR DEFECTS EXPERIENCED.

Only one major defect occured and that was on 7 August, 1942. The second section of the port main engine exhaust header piping started leaking badly and flooded numbers 5 and 6 cylinders. This showed up while the engine was stopped during a short period of lying to on surface at night. The welded seam at junction of header section and elbow was cracked open. Repairs were affected in 2 hours by peening the welded seam. This repair, of course, was only temporary and held sufficiently well that as long as the engine was running there seemed to be no danger of flooding any cylinders. To take care of any leakage during a dive there was a small drain fitted to the elbow of the section to permit draining after the engine was stopped. All other defects experienced were minor and readily repaired.

10. RADIO RECEPTION:

(a) The high frequency FOX schedules were good on one of the various bands at all times except occasional interruptions due to the antennae grounding out from salt water spray.

(b) The low frequency FOX schedules were good at all times. Night effect was noticeable but to no serious extent.

(c) The high frequency NERK series were excellent on 4235 kcs. but daytime frequencies afforded weak results.

(d) The low frequency intercept band (450 kcs) was very

ENCLOSURE (C)

CONFIDENTIAL

U.S.S. S-32 - REPORT OF THIRD WAR PATROL.

poor. Signals were heard on this band only once and too poorly to be copied.

RADIO TRANSMISSIONS:
(a) Transmissions were, for the greater part of the time, easily manageable at night on 4235 series. It was not always possible to communicate with NPM, nor any other particular shore station. NPR was very difficult to contact during the first part of the patrol. Daytime transmissions were made on 8470 and 16940 kcs., broadcast method, for no "R" method was possible. Shore stations utilized during patrol were NPC, NPG, NPM and NPR.

INTERFERENCE:
On two occasions there was enemy interference on NPM's high frequency FOX schedules. No interference was noticed on their low frequency schedules. There was always a great amount of interference noted on all 4235 series and particularly on 4235 kcs. during darkness. All interference was enemy origin consisting of Vs, dashes and garbled characters. Some times the enemy would call our shore stations. Whenever we opened up to send a message the enemy would attempt to interfere immediately by holding his transmitter key down or make long dashes.

CONSECUTIVE SERIALS:
(a) Last consecutive serial sent was CIPET in the first series and KIAM in the second series.
(b) Last consecutive series received was LAGER in the first series and DALL RIDGE in the second series.

11. SOUND CONDITIONS.
In both areas patrolled it appeared that sound conditions were excellent. This was not true when within a mile or two of the shore line of any of the islands. The rush of the surf and water falls could be heard over the JK, and would undoubltedly hamper good sound results.

The temperature gradient of the water was only one degree farenheit reduction from surface to a depth of 180 feet. This change occurred at 110 feet and then remained constant down to 180 feet. The average sea water temperature was 47 degrees F. The majority of operations were conducted in water greater than 500 fathoms. The sound equipment appears to be ultra-sensitive in these areas. During submerged operations in RATAM we heard explosions through the hull that were presumably the results of bombings of KISKA harbor about 35 miles distant.

ENCLOSURE (C)

CONFIDENTIAL

U.S.S. S-32 - REPORT OF THIRD WAR PATROL.

12. HEALTH and HABITABILITY.

The health of the officers and crew remained remarkably excellent throughout entire patrol. There was one case of tonsillitus that caused the man to stay in his bunk for three days before complete recovery. There were numerous head colds and coughs but all cleared up with no ill effects. Also numerous cases of constipation at start of patrol, but these cases were soon corrected.

This class submarine does not permit sufficient stowage spaces for more than a 30 days supply of blanced ration provisions. Although this patrol lasted 36 days the past 5 days we scraped for the remaining dregs of any food available. In spite of the fact we realised that the patrol may extend beyond a 30 day period and care was taken from the very beginning to conserve on provisions we considered ourselves lucky to eat well throughout the entire patrol. In this respect it is believed that the rations of vitamin pills do wonders toward maintenance of a high standard of health.

During all day submerged patrol periods the inside of the boat was practically a picture of a light rainfall. The sweating was greater than ever before experienced. This condition was not as bad later on during patrol, no doubt as a result of the battery temperature increase due to daily charges. It was too cold to attempt to use the air-conditioning plant to dry out the interior.

This vessel has been at sea 92 days out of the past 124 days. It is believed that considering the age of this vessel the crew has done remarkably well to provide constant maintenance under past conditions and remain in such good spirits and health.

13. Miles steamed enroute station - - - - -1100
Miles steamed from station - - - - - - 745
Total 1845 miles.

14. Fuel oil expended - 18,150.

15. Factors of endurance remaining:

TORPEDOES	FUEL	PROVISIONS	FRESH WATER	PERSONNEL
12	10,350	0 days	self sustaning	25 days

16. Orders were received from task group commander terminating this patrol, but lack of provisions would have justified returning from patrol in another 2 or 3 days at the most.

17. REMARKS:

(1) The commanding officer considers the following

alterations urgently required to place this vessel in an efficient condition for future patrols:

(a) Install Kleinschmidt evaporator.
(b) Install fathometer.
(c) Install radar.
(d) Install sanitary tanks.

Authorization has already been approved for (a), (b) and (c) above but not for (d).

(2) It is considered requisite to have the allowance changed in personnel to provide for one pharmacist mate. In past patrols there have been occasions when the need of a pharmacist mate was urgent and only by the maximum amount of luck were serious results avoided. Since the berthing situation in this class submarine is very acute, it is recommended that space can be provided for a pharmacist mate during patrol by leaving the [illegible] at the base

FC45/A16-3
Serial (01)

August 11, 1942.

CONFIDENTIAL

From: The Commander Submarine Squadron FORTY-FIVE.
To : The Commander Submarines, PACIFIC FLEET.

Subject: U.S.S. S-32 - Third Patrol Report.

1. The S-32 left San Diego on June 23rd and proceeded on patrol after two days in Dutch Harbor, returning on August 10th. The material condition of the S-32 was excellent and the engineer force were very ingenious in the repair of the one major defect that occurred.

2. The morale of the crew upon return from patrol was excellent. The factor of endurance remaining - Personnel - 25 days - is based solely on the stowage space available to carry a balanced ration to cover this period. This is an impossibility on this type submarine. A thirty day patrol period is considered the maximum for efficient performance of personnel in an S-class submarine.

3. It is recommended that the fathometer and radar be installed at the first opportunity. The Kleinschmidt evaporator is essential but not urgent. An alteration request will be initiated for the installation of a sanitary tank by this command.

4. The recommendation for a change in personnel to provide for a pharmacist's mate is concurred in and has been the subject of previous correspondence.

-10-

ENCLOSURE (C)

TG8.5/A16-3
Serial (06)

August 11, 1942.

CONFIDENTIAL

From: Commander Task Group Eight Point Five.
To : The Commander Submarines, Pacific Fleet.

Subject: War Patrol, U.S.S. S-32, report of.

Enclosure: (A) U.S.S. S-32, Report of Third War Patrol.
(B) Comsubron Forty-Five Conf. Ltr: FC45/A16-3, Ser. (01) dated Aug. 11, 1942.

1. This patrol extended for a period of thirty-six days, of which twenty-nine days were spent on station. The patrol, while terminated by orders of the Task Group Commander, had reached the limit of endurance with respect to provisions.

2. The assignment of the S-32 to an area north of Attu, with the duty of reporting weather during the second bombardment operation against Kiska, was a necessary feature of that operation. During the first Kiska operation it was found that adverse flying conditions prevented essential and timely weather reports from planes being relied upon. The problem invloved in making routine weather reports in an area largely occupied by the enemy was fully appreciated, and every effort made to avoid, in so far as practicable, compromise of the submarine's position.

3. A considerable part of this patrol was spent in confined waters in low visibility with currents of unknown set and drift. While a fathometer and radar would unquestionably have added materially to the effectiveness of this patrol, the Commanding Officer is to be congratulated on the thoroughness with which he covered the area. That his efforts were not repaid with attack opportunities is regrettable.

-11-

ENCLOSURE (C)

1st copy

FF12-10/A16-3(5) SUBMARINE FORCE, PACIFIC FLEET Rs

Serial 01235

DECLASSIFIED
CONFIDENTIAL

Care of Fleet Post Office,
San Francisco, California,
October 28, 1942.

3841
11 01092

COMSUBPAC PATROL REPORT NO. 81
U.S.S. S-32 - FOURTH WAR PATROL.

From: The Commander Submarine Force, Pacific Fleet.
To : Submarine Force, Pacific Fleet.

Subject: U.S.S. S-32 (SS137) - Report of Fourth War Patrol.

Enclosure: (A) Copy of ComTaskGroup 8.5 Conf. ltr. TG8.5/A16-3 Serial 030 of September 29, 1942.
(B) Copy of Comsubron 45 Conf. ltr. FC45/A16-3 Serial 033 of September 29, 1942.
(C) Copy of Subject War Patrol.

1. Enclosures (A), (B) and (C) are forwarded.

2. The ingenuity and skill displayed by the engineer's force of the S-32 in making repairs to the main engine air compressor should serve as an example of what can be accomplished with limited facilities when the necessity arises.

R. H. ENGLISH.

DISTRIBUTION
(35CM-42)
List III: SS.
Special:
P1(5), EN3(5), Z1(5)
Comsublant (2),
Comsubssowespac (2).

E. R. Swinburne
E. R. SWINBURNE,
Flag Secretary.

43840 FILMED

TG8.5/A16-3
Serial (030)

CONFIDENTIAL

Naval Operating Base,
Dutch Harbor, Alaska,
September 29, 1942.

From: The Commander Task Group Eight Point Five.
To : The Commander Submarines, Pacific Fleet.

Subject: U.S.S. S-32 - Report of Fourth War Patrol.

Enclosure: (A) Subject Report.

1. This patrol, covering a period of thirty-three days, of which twenty-seven were spent on station, was well conducted. Areas assigned were thoroughly exploited. Its unproductiveness was partially due to assignment for two weeks to an inactive area for protective scouting in connection with an amphibious operation.

2. Repair items will be accomplished during the current refit period, largely by Submarine Base and Repair Unit personnel, and ample time will be afforded for rest and relaxation of the officers and crew. The operating schedule of the S-class submarines in this area has been intensive. Morale and material conditions have been maintained at a uniformly excellent standard in the face thereof.

3. Enclosure (A) to subject Report, an excellent track chart, is being retained for planning purposes.

-1- ENCLOSURE (A)

FC45/A16-3
Serial (033)
CONFIDENTIAL

September 29, 1942.

From: The Commander Submarine Squadron Forty-Five.
To : The Commander Submarines, Pacific Fleet.

Subject: U.S.S. S-32 - Fourth War Patrol.

1. The Fourth War Patrol of the U.S.S. S-32 covered a period of thirty-three (33) days of which twenty-seven (27) were spent in patrol areas. More than half the days on station were spent in an area where enemy contacts were remote, but this defensive use of the S-32 was necessary to cover an amphibious operation. No enemy contacts were made.

2. Investigation of the leak in the after trim tank will be made and corrected if docking is not necessary. There are at present no docking facilities at this base. The other defects will be corrected during the present refit period.

3. During the last refit period the base was in the process of being established. The Repair Unit was newly arrived and inexperienced and it was necessary for the crews to do more work than will be required during this refit period. Adequate rest and relaxation can be furnished but recreation facilities are lacking.

4. The ingenuity and resourcefulness of the engineer's force in effecting major repairs and manufacturing spare parts was commendable and enabled the S-32 to remain on station until the completion of the patrol.

-1-

ENCLOSURE (B)

CONFIDENTIAL

Subject: U.S.S. S-32 - Report of Fourth War Patrol.

Period from: August 22, 1942 to September 23, 1942.

AREAS: ____

Operation Order: Commander Task Group 8.5 Operation Order No. 8-42. Commander Task Group 8.5 despatches 260905 and 281100 of August 1942; 141011 of September 1942.

NARRATIVE:

In accordance with Commander Task Group Eight Point Five Operation Order No. 8-42 and subsequent changes thereto the following report of the Fourth War Patrol of the U.S.S. S-32 is submitted.

Zone YOKE used for all times.

The greater part of daylight patrolling was carried out by this vessel while submerged to periscope depth. At night we had to lie to from three to four hours using both engines on battery charge.

As soon as one engine became available for propulsion we patrolled in the area under way on one engine while finishing the battery charge on the other. Ordinarily we had to submerge forty minutes before sunrise each day. During submerged patrol periscope depth was maintained and observations varied from continuous to not greater than ten minute intervals depending upon weather conditions. Length of daily submerged operations varied from fifteen to sixteen hours.

8/22/42 Departed DUTCH HARBOR for areas ____ and ____ at 1057. Joined by three planes acting as a coverage during passage through swept channel and westward to north of CAPE CHEERFUL.

Submerged at 1243 to check trim; surfaced at 1310.

Passed BOGOSLOF ISLAND abeam to port at 1613.

8/23/42 At 1501 sighted ship bearing 310 degrees true, distance 6 miles; changed course to intercept. Estimated course of ship 090 degrees true. Submerged to avoid detection and conduct approach. Ship recognized to be a large submarine. It was known that the TRITON was enroute DUTCH HARBOR but thought that her route would take her at least ten miles south of our track. We were unable to get within firing range of submarine but did get near enough to identify as our own fleet type submarine. Surfaced at 1605 to challenge but unsuccessful in visual communication. Continued course and speed enroute to patrol area; having decided the submarine was the TRITON.

- 1 - ENCLOSURE (C)

CONFIDENTIAL

Subject: U.S.S. S-32 - Report of Fourth War Patrol.

- -

8/24/42 At 0400 the barometer dropped suddenly and soon there after we ran into a storm and very heavy seas. Forced to slow to two thirds speed.

8/25/42 At 0110 sighted left tangent of SEMISOPOCHNOI ISLAND bearing 168 degrees true, estimated distance was eleven miles. At 0408 passed abeam of LITTLE SITKIN ISLAND, distance fifteen miles. Submerged at 0430 and decided to patrol just North of KHVOSTOF PASS in order to intercept any Japanese shipping reputedly using this route. Surfaced at 2000, lying too charging battery, position 6 miles North of HKVOSTOF PASS. Seas were very rough and visibility only fair. At 0011 received despatch from task group commanderestablishing new areas to be occupied by daylight 29 August 1942; our assignment Area ----. In order to make the best of our short stay in our present area I decided to progress towards KISKA along the SEGULA ISLAND - SIRIUS POINT - BULDIR ISLAND line.

8/26/42 Submerged at 0439 and decided to patrol just north of the line from SIRIUS POINT - SEGULA ISLAND. This route is supposed to be followed by a high per centage of Japanese shipping enroute ATTU to KISKA. At 0531 sound reported super-sonic pinging bearing approximately 350 degrees true. This pinging was manual and a code letter was interspersed about every two minutes. Periscope observ tions failed to reveal any surface craft. It is believed, as a result of this and past experiences, that the Japanese echo-ranging equipment can be heard at greater ranges than our own gear. This is either true or the water conditions in this area are such that sound carries to greater ranges than average. Sound reported propeller noises on bearing 150 degrees true. Course was changed to that bearing but periscope observ tions proved negative. We continued to hear super sonice pinging, manually, interspersed with the code signal "negat" for 5 hours. We finally decided the source was either a submarine or surface vessel beyond range of visibility. We thought surely we had a target but luck failed us again.

CONFIDENTIAL

Subject: U.S.S. S-32 - Report of Fourth War Patrol.

- -

8/27/42 Decided to patrol towards KISKA from a position North of SEGULA ISLAND. At 1412 heard a series of loud under water explosions that may have been the results of Army bombing KISKA HARBOR. Patrolled to within 1½ miles KISKA; periscope observations negative. Surfaced at 2018 just four miles north of SIRIUS POINT, KISKA and charged batteries. Visibility excellent.

8/28/42 At 0211 received task group commanders despatch ordering us to proceed at best speed to area ____ and observe AMCHITKA ISLAND for indications of enemy activities thereon. Set course for new area immediately. The despatch ordering this shift was received 3 hours after its origination hence I was prevented from arriving in [illegible] prior daylight. I was warned about increased enemy air activity in this area so was hesitant to travel on the surface anymore than necessary. I surmised that our observations of AMCHITKA were desired to be undetected so the decision was reached to dive soon after day light and proceed into [illegible] around the northern point of LITTLE SITKIN while submerged. At 0411 sighted LITTLE SITKIN bearing 150 degrees true. At 0521 submerged and continued into area. I had been given two days for this reconnaissance so I felt there was ample time to conduct it in the manner decided upon. At 1700 arrived two miles off northern coast of AMCHITKA. Thorough observation along this section negative. During night decided to proceed to a point about four miles north of CONSTANTINE HARBOR in order to observe it the first thing in the morning.

During the afternoon a leak developed in the after trim tank and it became necessary to fully flood this tank. The ship's compensation then resulted in placing 18000 pounds in forward trim. The space left in forward trim would only accommodate water for one torpedo reload. It was realized that this situation may limit any future operations in action but the rupture in the after trim tank may cause a disaster during any depth charge attack. The advantage of proper depth control, it was decided, out weighted the availability of a second reload. Fuel oil suction was shifted to the forward group in order to permit daily removal of water from the forward trim tank and therby improve the situation slowly.

CONFIDENTIAL

Subject: U.S.S. S-32 - Report of Fourth War Patrol.

- -

8/29/42 Submerged at 0411 and during the day conducted a thorough search of CONSTANTINE HARBOR, KIRILOF BAY and all along the northeast coast of the south east portion of AMCHITKA ISLAND. There were no indications of enemy activities of any nature. Surfaced at 2000 and sent a despatch to task group commander informing of the results of our reconnaissance. Set course for area ____. Sudden storm set in at 2300 and we were forced to slow to two-thirds speed.

8/30/42 Conducted surface patrol in area ____. Position doubtful since bucking mountainous seas all last night. Finally at 1718 sighted land 240 degrees true distance four miles. Identified land to be GARELOI ISLAND. At 1620 sighted TANAGA ISLAND and obtained good fix.

8/31/42 to 9/13/42 Conducted daily submerged patrols and nightly surface patrols in area ____. Since the occupation of this area is for the purpose of acting as a protective scout covering army shore operations I decided to patrol on a north - south line along meridian of longitude 178-20 west. In this manner it was believed the best protective scouting could be maintained. Our patrolling would take us from the northern limit of the area to within two miles of TANAGA ISLAND. Upon some days we shifted our north and south patrol line to extend to the north of GARELOI ISLAND in order to search for movements of the enemy through both AMCHITKA and TANAGA PASSES.

At 1347 September 3, sighted two Army bombers type B-24 on course 090 degrees true flying just north of TANAGA ISLAND at an altitude of about 5000 feet. These planes were apparently returning from KISKA.

At 0425 September 8, just prior to our twilight diving time, we sighted a plane one mile away coming directly towards us at an altitude of about 1500 feet.
This plane was heard by one of the lookouts just prior sighting. We dove immediately and altered our course 090 degrees. We thought the pilot may have sighted us but no bombs were dropped. We were unable to identify the plane under the visibility conditions for it just appeared as a dark object. Under conditions in this area where the ship is outlined by the phosphorescent properties of the sea we took no chances of being readily sighted due to this effect.

On 11 September the port main engine air compressor failed to function properly. The engine was placed out of commission and repairs undertaken lasting through a period of fifteen hours. At 1500 on 11 September the port main engine was back in commission.

CONFIDENTIAL

Subject: U.S.S. S-32 - Report of Fourth War Patrol.

- -

9/13/42 At 2347 received orders from task group commander to proceed immediately to and patrol area ---. Large scale army air attacks on KISKA were scheduled starting the morning of 14 September. We were to observe exits from KISKA Harbor leading into area --- and destroy any shipping leaving KISKA HARBOR through these passes, as a result of the air bombardments.

9/14/42 At 0200 entered area --- and proceeded towards the junction of RAT ISLAND and OGLALA PASSES. It was decided to patrol this sector of area as the best position for accomplishing present mission.

9/15/42 Extended patrol as far northwest into RAT ISLAND PASS as area allowed in order to observe for any enemy use of KHVOSTOV PASS. It had been determined in the past that the enemy had been using this pass enroute to and from KISKA HARBOR. Observations were negative and visibility (surface) was excellent. At 0957 and 1007 heard distant explosions; source undetermined.

9/16/42 Repeated patrol in sector same as yesterday. Results negative. It was found fairly easy to maintain an excellent periscope search of KHVOSTOV PASS in spite of varying currents and not too good depth control at periscope depth.

9/16/42 to 9/19/42 Patrolled in sector of area where OGLALA and RAT ISLAND PASSES meet. Visibility was consistently poor and never again clear enough to venture well up into RAT ISLAND PASS. Navigating in this pass is perorarious to say the least.

9/20/42 9/21/42 At dark departed area --- for DUTCH HARBOR via AMCHITKA PASS in accordance with despatch orders received from task group commander.

9/22/42 At 1900 sighted two ships about 30 degrees on the starboard bow distance approximately 4000 yards, speed 9 knots on course 190° T. Immediately turned for surface approach. Determined silhouette to be U.S. Destroyer (4 stacker) leading a single merchantman. Changed course to left to clear them.

-5- ENCLOSURE (C)

CONFIDENTIAL

Subject: U.S.S. S-32 - Report of Fourth War Patrol.

- -

The destroyer passed our starboard beam about 800 yards and apparently did not sight us. When we were well on her starboard quarter she turned to her starboard. At this time I decided to challenge her to make certain that she would not suddenly open fire. As soon as we challenged she fired a green verys' star and simultaneously answered our challenge correctly. We then exchanged calls and she proved to be the USS HUMPHREYS. I could not understand the greenverys' star for the proper signal by that method was two white stars. Her signal therefore must have been for the merchantman for she changed course, at that time, to her port away from us. At 1915 we resumed course.

WEATHER

(a) Enroute patrol areas -- and ---. Foggy, heavy seas. Wind and seas from southwest.
(b) KISKA areas -- and --. Average visibility was five miles. Visibility at times was maximum. Heavy seas were encountered two of the three days we occuppied these areas. Winds were of forces from fifteen to twenty five knots from southwest.
(c) Area -- . Fair to excellent visibility in day time; usually foggy or misty at night. Moderate to heavy seas from the northwest throughout area. Moderate winds and occasional rain.
(d) Area -- . Heavy seas and strong winds from the northwest encountered while enroute this area from --. In the area there was twenty five miles visibility seventy five per cent of the day time. Nights were usually misty. Seas were moderate except off and in TANAGA PASS where they were heavy.
(e) Enroute DUTCH HARBOR. The weather was fair except for last day when we ran through a gale from the east. Visibility during this gale varied from one half to two miles. This gale continued until after we arrived at Dutch Harbor.

TIDAL DATA

(a) Enroute patrol areas KISKA --- and ---. Set 070 degrees to 115 degrees true; drift 1.0 knot.
(b) KISKA areas -- and --. Set 075 degrees true; drift 1.1 knots.

CONFIDENTIAL

Subject: U.S.S. S-32 - Report of Fourth War Patrol.

- -

(c) Area ---. Average set 190 degrees true; drift 0.8 knots. In RAT ISLAND PASS and off KHVOSTOF PASS the seas were always from the northwest, yet the average current was set 020 degrees true; drift 0.9 knots. Depth control in RAT ISLAND PASS was good and easily controlled. Very peculiar currents were experienced southeast and southwest of SEMISOPOCHNOI ISLAND. On the southwest side with seas from 340 degrees true the set was 000 degrees true; drift 1.5 to 2.5 knots. On the southeast side with seas from due north the set was 160 degrees true; drift 2 to 3 knots.

(d) Area ---. Off TANAGA PASS the set was 180 degrees true or 000 degrees true; drift 1 to 2 knots. North of GARELOI ISLAND the set was 145 degrees true; drift 0.6 knots. North of TANAGA ISLAND the set was 125 degrees true; drift 0.5 knots.

(e) Enroute RATAM to DUTCH HARBOR. Current experienced was set 080 degrees true; drift 0.5 knots.

4. NAVIGATIONAL AIDS

Good fixes were obtained using any of the following island tangents; SEGULA, KISKA, LITTLE SITKIN, DAVIDOF, KHVOSTOF and PYRAMID. RAT ISLAND did not give such good results. The large flat top rock at the south eastern end of RAT ISLAND is 1000 yards, bearing 275 degrees true from its charted position. This rock is an excellent landmark when within ten miles of it.

There is an uncharted large rock several hundred yards off the point on SEMISOPOCHNOI ISLAND which bears 162 degrees true, distance 5.3 miles from TUMAN POINT.

Navigation around SEMISOPOCHNOI ISLAND in poor visibility is very dangerous because of strong currents with their peculiar sets, as described in paragraph 3 (c).

The south tangent of GARELOI ISLAND appears to be about four (4) miles further north than its charted position.

A high and very conspicuous water fall on the north coast of TANAGA ISLAND was plotted and found to be 2.8 miles bearing 025 degrees true from the volcano. This water fall is an excellent land mark.

5. NONE SIGHTED

CONFIDENTIAL

Subject: U.S.S. S-32 - Report of Fourth War Patrol.

- -

6. AIRCRAFT SIGHTED

DATE	TIME	TYPE	POSITION	COURSE	ALTITUDE
3 Sept.	1347	B-24	Lat. 52-00 N. Long. 178-05 W.	090	4000 ft.
3 Sept.	1347	B-24	Lat. 52-00 N. Long. 178-05 W.	090	4000 ft.
8 Sept.	0425	Unknown	Lat. 52-10 N.	135	1500 ft.
10 Sept.	1420	B-24	Lat 52-10 N. Long. 178-08 W	270	4000 ft.
11 Sept.	1310	B-25	Lat 52-12N. Long. 178-12W	090	3000 ft.
13 Sept.	1540	P-38	Lat. 52-05 N. Long. 178-10W.	090	2000 ft.
22 Sept	0840	PBY	Lat. 53-38 N. Long. 171-30W.	260	2000 ft.

7. MAJOR DEFECTS EXPERIENCED

(a) On 28 August 1942 it was found that a major leak had developed in the after trim tank. It was believed that the location of this leak was in the shaft tubing. It was necessary to carry this tank completely flooded from that time on as explained in the narrative for that day.

(b) During the battery charge on the morning of 3 September 1942 a strange noise was heard eminating from the port main engine clutch. The engine was stopped and an inspection revealed the following derangement:

The connecting links between No. 1 shoe and counter weight were broken. BuShips Drawing No. 123-0-050 and EB Co. Dr. No. 8EB15-19, part "D". There were no spares on board so a new set were manufactured using brass stock; installed and provided satisfactory operation thereafter. This work was done during the submerged run on 4 September.

(c) Port main engine air compressors. BuShips Dr. No. 123-0-0265. During the battery charge on the evening of 10 September 1942 the port main engine air compressor failed to keep sufficient pressure. It was decided that this was probably due to wear or breakage of the second stage ring.

CONFIDENTIAL

Subject: U.S.S. S-32 - Report of Fourth War Patrol.

- -

Starting the ~~morning of 11~~ September the air compressor was completed disassembled and removed from the engine. Three broken piston rings were found on the third stage pistons, and two broken rings on the second stage piston. A hole about 3/8 inch in diameter was found in the crown of the first stage piston..

The first stage rings were in satisfactory condition. The forward discharge valve of the first stage was completely severed. Since the second stage ring grooves had veen widened during a navy yard overhaul and only standard size rings were available on board as spares it was necessary to machine two new rings down to replace each of the broken rings. Our auxiliaryman did an excellent job on this. The hole in the first stage piston was repaired using a 3/8 inch counter sunk screw and lead and leather washers. The third stage rings were renewed. The forward first stage discharge valve was renewed.

The air compressor was completely reassembled by 1500 on 11 September and upon surfacing that evening functioned satisfactorily.

(d) Main engine clutches, Buships Dr. No. 123-0-050, EB Co No. 8EB15-19, parts "B" and "D".

During the charge on the evening of 17 September 1942 both main engine clutches started getting noisy. The engines were stopped and an inspection revealed that some of the connecting links, part "D" had lengthened (not broken) and allowed the counter weights to chatter. Further inspections revealed that four of the shoe brackets, part "B", in the starboard clutch and one in the port clutch were broken. This, at first, seemed most serious for there was a danger of the counter weights moving out to the clutch rim and causing severe damage and disabled engines. There was no material on board of sufficient size to allow manufacturing new brackets and no spares carried. The clutches were not disassembled or touched in any manner for it was feared that if the broken brackets were removed they could not be replaced again. Although noisy and undoubtedly a large torsional stress caused by this condition the clutches were left alone with the hope that no serious results would occur during the remainder of the trip returning to DUTCH HARBOR.

10. RADIO RECEPTION

(a) On low frequency NPM faded out about 1500 GCT., the 7000 Kcs band became weak and the 14000 Kcs band proved very weak. Reception between the hours 1400 and 1600 GCT proved to be poor but not to the extent that any of the FOX schedules were missed.

(b) Nothing was heard on the 450 Kcs watch.

- 9 - ENCLOSURE (C)

CONFIDENTIAL

Subject: U.S.S. S-32 - Report of Fourth War Patrol.

- -

10. RADIO RECEPTION (Continued)

(c) As a whole, better results were obtained guarding NPG than were previously guarding NPM. This was due to the 7000 Kcs band providing a more suitable frequency during night hours.
(d) Reception while submerged proved unsatisfactory. At 48 feet the signals were inconsistent. At 53 feet signals faded out completely. At 42 feet, depending upon time of day and ship's course a fair amount of traffic could be copied. It seems much better for reception while submerged to be heading either towards or away from the geographical location of the station transmitting.

RADIO TRANSMISSIONS:
(a) One night transmissions was cleared immediately on 4235 kcs and communications on this occasion were excellent.
(b) One day time transmission was made with difficulty but after several attempts the despatch was cleared to NPG on 4235 kcs.

INTERFERENCE:

During the first part of the patrol there was quite a bit of Japanese interference on 7065 kcs but even so there was less interference while guarding NPG than while guarding NPM.

CONSECUTIVE SERIALS:
(a) Last consecutive serial sent was NOBLE.
(b) Last consecutive serial received was COMET.

11. SOUND CONDITIONS

Sound conditions seemed to be excellent as previously reported for these areas but due to lack of visual targets no accurate information can be given. The sound gear functioned properly and seemed to be particularly sensitive in these waters away from shore.

12. HEALTH AND HABITABILITY

Coughs and colds were very prevalent. Several of the crew had colds which defied treatment throughout the entire patrol. There was no sickness that required relief from duty. There were occasional cases of constipation but not as bad as during the last patrol. There were frequent cases of headaches and one bad case of athletes' foot.

Recreation consisted of card games and reading. A fair supply of magazines and books, luckily obtained just prior departure on patrol, was read completely. A limited amount of candy was rationed throughout the patrol, and helped to vary the steady diet.

CONFIDENTIAL

Subject: U.S.S. S-32 - Report of Fourth War Patrol.

12. HEALTH AND HABITABILITY (Continued)

The spirit of the crew was excellent but dropped noticeably towards the end of the patrol.

This vessel completed a 35 day patrol in these waters followed by a 10 day refit period just before commencing the present patrol. During this refit period repair work prevented the majority of the crew from obtaining sufficient rest and relaxation. Towards the end of this patrol the effect of the strain became very noticeable. The men had lost their usual pep; they became less efficient, listless and nervous. Nearly all had lost considerable weight and their complexions were very poor. At the end of this patrol the officers and crew appeared to be in a general run down condition. They show very much the need of a good rest and relaxation before another patrol.

13. Miles steamed enroute station-------------- 715
Miles steamed from station----------------- 550
Total 1265 miles.

14. Fuel oil expended-------------------------- 17,250 gallons.

15. Factors of endurance remaining:

Torpedoes	Fuel	Provisions	Fresh Water	Personnel
12	11,500	7 days	Self-Sustaining	0 days

16. Orders were received from task group commander terminating this patrol.

17. REMARKS:
NONE

18. A track chart showing complete track of this vessel in patrol areas is enclosed wherwith as enclosure "A".

 ENCLOSURE (C)

1st Copy

80279

FF12-10/A16-3(5) SUBMARINE FORCE, PACIFIC FLEET Rs

Serial 01361

Care of Fleet Post Office,
San Francisco, California,
November 30, 1942.

DECLASSIFIED
~~CONFIDENTIAL~~

COMSUBPAC PATROL REPORT NO. 99
U.S.S. S-32 - FIFTH WAR PATROL.

From: The Commander Submarine Force, Pacific Fleet.
To : Submarine Force, Pacific Fleet.

Subject: U.S.S. S-32 - Report of Fifth War Patrol.

Enclosure (A) ComTaskGroup 8.5 Conf ltr TG8.5/A16-3 Serial 040 of October 30, 1942.
(B) Comsubron 45 Conf ltr FC34/A16-3 Serial 055 of October 31, 1942.
(C) Copy of Subject Report.

1. The Commanding Officer of the U.S.S. S-32 displayed commendable initiative and judgment in his attack on the two enemy freighters at anchor in MUSASHI WAN.

2. The Commander Submarine Force, Pacific Fleet, concurs with the remarks of Commander Task Group 8.5 contained in enclosure (C).

3. The Commanding Officer, officers and men of the U.S.S. S-32 are congratulated on having inflicted the following damage on the enemy.

DAMAGED

1 freighter - 6,000 Tons

R. H. ENGLISH.

DISTRIBUTION:
(35CM-42)
List III: SS.
Special:
P1(5), EN3(5), Z1(5)
Consublant (2), X3(1)
Consubsowespac (2)

E. R. Swinburne
E. R. SWINBURNE,
Flag Secretary.

RECEIVED — FILES
Room 465
DEC 22 1942

Finished—Nomm—File

FILMED
87582

(SC)A16-3(2)

TG8.5/A16-3
Serial 040

October 30, 1942.

CONFIDENTIAL

From: The Commander Task Group Eight Point Five.
To : The Commander Submarines, Pacific Fleet.

Subject: U.S.S. S-32 - Report of Fifth War Patrol.

Enclosure: (A) Original and one copy of subject report.

1. This comparatively short patrol was dictated by the time available between the completion of the refit on October 7 and the scheduled departure of the S-32 on November 1 for SAN DIEGO for upkeep and Sound School Services. The patrol was further shortened by a fueling discrepancy of 9000 gallons. In view of the limited time available, the decision to continue the patrol, upon discovery of the discrepancy four days out from base, with the prospect of returning from PARAMUSHIRU on one engine, is considered indicative of a commendably tenacious attitude. That this decision was rewarded by the ship making her first contacts with the enemy and that it resulted in the infliction of damage thereon is most gratifying.

2. The attack upon two freighters at anchor in shallow water in [illegible]LASHI WAN was carefully planned, including the destruction of classified material. The attack was boldly executed, being carried through in spite of unexpectedly grounding upon a sand bar with the probable disclosure of the submarine's presence. While, from the data, assuming normal torpedo performance, hits on both freighters were to be expected, there is no conclusive evidence of hits upon the second target. Furthermore, although observed to be burning and settling, the sinking of the first target cannot be assumed, in view of the shallow depth of water in which she was anchored and the proximity of the shore for beaching. It is considered, therefore, that the S-32 should be credited with one 6000-ton freighter damaged.

3. The decision of the Commanding Officer to break off the attack on the freighter on October 17, on the grounds that he believed her to be Russian is not criticized. Since the difficult problem presented in the northwest Pacific by reason of Russian shipping will confront the commanding officers of submarine frequently, and since there is evidence of Japanese shipping following the Russian route from and to a point northwest of KISKA, comment thereon is in order, however. In recognition of this problem, and in accordance with instructions from higher authority, the Task Group Commander has directed attack upon all unidentifiable

-1- ENCLOSURE "A"

CONFIDENTIAL

Subject: U.S.S. S-32 - Report of Fifth War Patrol.

- -

ships if there is a reasonable presumption that they are enemy. Questioning of the masters of Russian merchant ships stopping at DUTCH HARBOR has failed to establish any standard procedure with respect to colors or other identifying marks, or with respect to lights shown at night. During daylight, in waters in which enemy shipping is to be expected, failure to show colors or other indications of nationality, such as colors painted up on the side, is considered to raise an initial presumption of enemy character. Likewise during darkness, failure to show normal running lights or to show illuminated colors furnishes grounds for such a presumption. Against this initial presumption the commanding officer at the periscope or on the bridge must weigh such factors as the type, the general lines, the personnel about the decks, and so forth. It is well for commanding officers, before reporting for patrol in the northwest Pacific and the Bering Sea, to give careful consideration to this problem, to the end that they will not be handicapped during the attack by indecision in the matter and that by the soundness of their decisions they will prevent enemy ships from attaining immunity by following the tracks of neutral shipping.

4. The reported fuel discrepancy is being thoroughly investigated to prevent a recurrence. The annoying experience reported in paragraph 18, of having radio transmissions prolonged by an operator at NPG refusing to take a despatch upon the grounds of erroneous encipherment is being made the subject of a report to that station.

5. By copy hereof the Commanding Officer, Officers, and crew of the S-32 are congratulated on the damage inflicted upon the enemy.

 ENCLOSURE "A"

FC34/A16-3
Serial 055

October 31, 1942.

<u>CONFIDENTIAL</u>

From: The Commander Submarine Squadron Forty-Five.
To : The Commander Submarines, Pacific Fleet.

Subject: U.S.S. S-32 - Fifth War Patrol.

1. The Fifth War Patrol of the S-32 covered a period of nineteen (19) days of which nine (9) days were spent in patrol areas. The patrol was terminated to permit the S-32 to depart for San Diego, as scheduled, for Sound School services, overhaul, and training.

2. The decision of the Commanding Officer to complete his assigned mission at reduced speed in spite of the fuel discrepancy was a sound decision and proved to be well worth any risk by the resulting damage inflicted on the enemy.

3. Investigation of the fuel discrepancy discloses that a tanker fueled the base tanks a day prior to the fueling of the S-32. The fueling line holds 6000 gallons of fuel and it is believed this line was full of water. The discharge was tested by sight before fueling, but the first thief sample was not taken until about an hour after fueling commenced. The descrepancy is attributed to the fuel in the filling line and to undetected water in number three main ballast tank. Steps have been taken to eliminate any further fuel discrepancies.

4. The S-32 returned in excellent material condition. The after trim tank was inspected after the Fourth Patrol and no leak could be found. Further investigation will be made during docking.

5. The Commander Submarine Squadron Forty-Five congratulates the Commanding Officer, officers, and crew for their well-conducted and successful patrol.

-1- ENCLOSURE "B"

CONFIDENTIAL

Subject: U.S.S. S-32 - Report of Fifth War Patrol.

- -

PERIOD FROM: October 8-27, 1942.

OPERATION ORDER: Commander TASK GROUP 8.5 OPERATION ORDER 21-42 and DESPATCH 230235 Of OCTOBER, 1942.

PROLOGUE: Arrived DUTCH HARBOR on September 23, 1942, from FOURTH WAR PATROL. Commenced refit on September 24, 1942, by Submarine Repair Unit assisted by ship's force. Completed refit on October 7, 1942. A very thorough main engine clutch overhaul job was done by repair unit. This repair unit accomplished excellent work and permitted the ship's crew to get sufficient rest and relaxation during refit period. Readiness for sea on October 8, 1942. Not depermed nor wiped; no training period.

1419 William 10/8/42 — 1. NARRATIVE:
Departed DUTCH HARBOR for areas assigned in accordance with Commander Task Group Operation Order 21-42. Air coverage until clear of swept channel. Surface escort by YP-400. Storm coming up from the east; seas heavy with long high swells. At 1530 changed zone time to plus eleven.

1454 Xray 10/8/42 — Cleared swept channel and at 1527 submerged for trim. The seas were very rough and our surface escort was having great trouble in maintaining steady course and speed thereby endangering us, hence we were unable to get a satisfactory trim dive.

-1- ENCLOSURE "C"

CONFIDENTIAL

Subject: U.S.S. S-32 - Report of Fifth War Patrol.

- -

Surfaced at 1539. The after trim tank gave evidence of leaking in spite of tests and examinations during our refit period showing no leak. At 1556 sent message to escort YP-400 releasing her from duty assigned. At 1700 cleared AKUTAN PASS. At 1719 made trim dive proved us to be either heavier than usual or to have a faulty auxiliary tank guage float. We finally decided the gauge was in error after dicussion with fueling gang who had checked fueling carefully and all tests indicated full amount reserve fuel on board. After trim tank had to be carried full as during our last war patrol, due to leaks under pressure. This again prevents more than 1½ torpedo reloads. In emergency we can dump water into the torpedo room bilges and thus get maximum reloads. At 1741 surfaced and went ahead at two thirds speed both engines, in accordance instructions, to conserve fuel for this long distance patrol.

0709 Xray 10/9/42 — Sighted Navy PBY plane bearing 000 degrees true, distance three (3) miles. Exchanged recognition signals.

1040 Xray — Sighted Navy PBY plane bearing 275 degrees true, distance twelve miles. We were undetected and plane disappeared heading North.

1055 Xray — Sighted ship bearing 270 degrees true, distance ten miles. Later proved to be sail class submarine undoubtedly the Sail 28 returning from patrol. Exchange of recognition signals unsuccessful due to distance.

1207 Xray — Training dive, surfacing at 1252; battle surface and fired 5 service rounds from deck gun and one pan .30 calibre from machine gun.

0711Xray 10/11/42 — Sighted plane bearing 070 degrees true, distance 4 miles heading toward us - unable to identify for certain but may be Army B-26. Dove immediately. Surfaced at 0723; plane not in sight.

CONFIDENTIAL

Subject: U.S.S. S-32 - Report of Fifth War Patrol.

- -

1202 Xray Sighted Navy PBY plane bearing 300 degrees true, distance 5 miles on course east. Plane did not detect us. At 1700 changed zone to plus twelve.

0700 Yoke 10/12/42 Ran out of reserve fuel in number 3 main ballast tank. This showed a fuel loss 9000 gallons. This had been suspected but we could not really believe such a discrepancy because the fueling was handled properly and tests were made during fueling process for presence of water. The only answer surmised was that the oil king at DUTCH HARBOR may have been receiving fuel from a tanker at the same time we were taking on fuel and between our checks we received water due to this double fueling. This fuel loss will shorten our stay around [illegible] to a day or two depending upon the weather. An estimate of the situation should allow us to reach the [illegible] and remain several days and return using two thirds speed on both engines enroute and two thirds speed on one engine returning and have a small factor of safety. This we intend to do realizing that weather will play an important part.

0815 Yoke Sighted Navy PBY plane bearing 220 degrees true, distance 10 miles. Plane turned towards us; recognition signals exchanged but he later made us feel uncomfortable by circling four times entirely too close - several times appearing to be on a bombing approach. We did not like it much. At 2400 changed time to zone minus twelve and date to October 14, 1942.

0611 Mike Sighted CAPE WRANGELL, ATTU ISLAND, bearing 340 degrees true distance 25 miles. Approached near enough to be certain of no off-lying vessels and then commenced patrol along rhumb line from CAPE WRANGELL to HOROMUSHIRO.

1000 Mile 10/15/42 Changed time to zone minus eleven. At 1029 submerged for training and surfaced at 1048.

10/16/42 Patrolled on surface.

0510 Love 10/17/42 Sighted single steady white light bearing 260 degrees true. It was the beginning of twilight and we were soon to be outlined against the horizon in the east so we closed as rapidly as possible on the surface until we thought detection soon probable and at 0551 submerged for approach. The white light was burning well forward on the bow of a freighter. Battle stations submerged. Description of vessel is as follows: (a) Plumb bow. (b) Counter Stern. (c) Three island broken deck.

(d) Two high masts.
(e) Two kingposts, just forward and abaft bridge structure.
(f) One stack (high).
(g) Lightly loaded.

A search of merchant vessel plates did not permit us to definitely identify the vessel. Decision was reached to break off the attack at 0632 for the following reasons:

(1) Believed to be a RUSSIAN ship.
  (a) Steering a route probably used by Russian Merchantmen enroute VLADIVOSTOK to PETROPAVLOVSK or DUTCH HARBOR.
  (b) Appeared similar to type shown on page 23 of O.N.I. number 208.
  (c) Lightly loaded.
  (d) Not zig-zagging.
  (e) Burning one steady white light well forward and this may be required of Russian ships by the Japanese while in their waters.

0830 Love Sighted PARAMUSHIRO to.

1328 Love Sighted ship bearing 260 degrees true distance 4 miles, angle on the bow 95 degrees starboard on northerly course. Went to battle stations submerged and changed course to 310 degrees true. Attempted to intercept at high speed but vessel drew slowly away. Description of this ship, believed to be Japanese is as follows:

(a) Raked bow.
(b) Three island.
(c) Cruiser stern.
(d) Two masts.
(e) One stack at height even with bridge structure and close abaft.

From sketch shown in "German and Italian Merchantmen and Raiders in the Pacific", serial number 0786216 of October 18, 1942, on page 21 it is believed quite possible that this vessel was the "MANYO MARU". At 1359 broke off attack; unable to intercept. At 1420 it was observed that this vessel changed course to enter KASHIWABARA WAN. At 1855 Love, surfaced off the coast of PARAMUSHIRU and charged battery.

2301 Love Secured one engine from battery charge and went ahead at two thirds speed one engine on course 230 degrees true. Decision was made to patrol off the entrance to MUSASHI WAN and ONEKOTAN KAIKYO. During night destroyed secret and confidential registered publications to prevent their falling into enemy hands in case of our destruction in salvageable waters.

CONFIDENTIAL

Subject: U.S.S. S-32 Report of Fifth War Patrol

- -

It will be necessary to operate in depths of less than 20 fathoms in order to thoroughly reconnoiter MUSASHI Wan or get in real close to land.

0516 Love 10/18/42 Sighted steady white light bearing 345 degrees true and commenced approach on the surface. A long low black outline was soon made out under the white light; appeared only several thousand yards distance so submerged at 0552 because it was getting light in the east and we could easily be detected. At 0555 changed course to 350 degrees true and thought the object sighted was a large submarine. Approached slowly to allow for better light conditions. At 0644 identified object to be long breakwater extending out from KURABU ZAKI to the reefs lying nearby. Altered course to clear reefs and bring us south of the harbor.

0704 Love Sighted two ships in MUSASHI WAN apparently at anchor bearing north. Decided to observe for movements and presence of more ships, hoping some would proceed out of the harbor.

0725 Love Apparently ships are not preparing to leave harbor so decided to go in after them. The chart shows 10 fathoms of water within 1000 yards of their assumed position. No real evidence of any contact mine fields (absence of mine sweepers); no surface or air patrols sighted even though ONI reports show a large air field here; so believe our chances good to enter slowly for attack. Current now flooding at 2 knots, set 300 degrees true. Commenced approach. Decided to work northwest until we could attack from the west or southwest and fire two torpedoes at each ship, depth setting of six (6) feet. Both vessels appear to be about 5000 - 6000 ton freighters similar to plate #98 "HAKODATE MARU" shown in pamphlet "Recognition of Japanese Merchantmen". Rigged for depth charge.

0945 Love Sound reported high speed screws bearing north and southwest of us but periscope searches revealed nothing. Considered we would be in firing position at 1031. The surface was very calm so periscope exposures had to be infrequent and very short. Tubes ready for firing at 1021 Love.

1023 Love Took periscope look for final check up and while looking we struck an unchartered sand bar and were suddenly angled up 10 degrees, seemingly out of control, depth gauge showing 32 feet. I decided to fire as soon as possible since we were apparently sighted showing our periscope shears, bow and possibly our whole bridge structure.

CONFIDENTIAL

Subject: U.S.S. S-32 Report of Fifth War Patrol

- -

1023 Love (cont'd)

The next few seconds we slid over bar, took a down angle, at high speed and regained control somewhat.

1025 Love Fired 2 torpedoes at each ship; changed course to the left with full rudder and full speed to 220 degrees true. Maneuvered at high speed and varying courses to clear harbor. Two dull explosions were heard by men in the radio shack, engine room and motor room about two minutes after firing first torpedo, and about 17 seconds apart. Remained as deep as possible while proceeding from harbor. Made torpedo reload.

1045 Love Came to periscope depth to observe damage. Right hand ship was afire amidship below bridge structure and had settled somewhat. Dark brown smoke was pouring out from her starboard side near the water line and billows of light gray smoke was massed near the water line on each side of the dark smoke area. Since she was anchored in shallow water she may have been resting on the bottom. The left hand ship was mostly obscured by the right hand ship and no evidence of damage to her was noticeable but torpedo tracks observed heading for each ship. It is probable that there were two hits on the right hand vessel but from observed torpedo wakes there should have been a hit on each. After this observation and a look for signs of enemy AS measures (negative) we went to 80 feet and proceeded out of harbor.

1205 Love Secured from battle stations and commenced periscope patrol remainder of the day, course east out of ONEKOTAN KAIKYO.

1527 Love Sighted smoke and then the tops of a two masted vessel bearing 180 degrees true, distance about 9 miles course approximately 270 degrees true. Checked her speed and found her too far away and making about 10 knots so did not attempt approach.

1848 Love Surfaced went ahead two-thirds speed on one engine and charged battery on the other. Set course 090 degrees true enroute DUTCH HARBOR due to fuel shortage and time limit. Decision was made to cover route leading from KISKA to ONEKOTAN KAIKYO.

1303 Love
10/19/42 Sighted Japanese destroyer of the "SHIGURE" class bearing 000 degrees true distance 10,000 yards, course 095 degrees true.

CONFIDENTIAL

Subject: U.S.S. S-32 Report of Fifth War Patrol

- -

1307 Love — Submerged, changed course to 060 degrees true and commenced approach. The destroyer speed was about 15 knots. She drew ahead rapidly and then changed course to 125 degrees true. The nearest we could get was about 6500 yards and she finally crossed our bow and disappeared without any further course change, bearing 100 degrees true. This destroyer was apparently not heading for any particular port and was assumed to be out looking for us or on a regular patrol. Distance to PARAMUSHIRU is only 100 miles.

1419 Love — Surfaced and continued course and speed. Destroyer not in sight; horizon misty, visibility fair.

10/20/42 — Patrolling on surface along rhumb line from KURABU ZAKI to point

2050 Love 10/21/42 — Cleared our despatch to task group commander reporting arrival time at Meridian 170 degrees east.

10/22/42 10/23/42 — Patrolling on surface; making early morning and evening dives daily until arrival DUTCH HARBOR. At 2000 love changed time to zone minus twelve. At 2400 mike changed zone time to plus twelve and retained same date, 23 October.

0847 Yoke 10/23/42 — Sighted Navy PBY plane bearing 050 degrees true, course 270 degrees true, distance twelve (12) miles and altitude about 3000 ft. Apparently plane crew failed to sight us and disappeared on same course at 0900 yoke.

1100 Yoke 10/23/42 — Arrived at point number 63 and commenced return to DUTCH HARBOR along route through odd numbered points and AKUTAN PASS.

0723 Yoke 10/24/42 — Sighted Navy PBY plane bearing 000 degrees true, course 260 degrees true, distance ten (10) miles and altitude about 1000 feet. Apparently plane crew failed to sight us and disappeared on same course bearing 305 degrees true.

0100 Yoke 10/25/42 — Changed zone time to plus eleven.

CONFIDENTIAL

Subject: U.S.S. S-32 Report of Fifth War Patrol

2015 Xray — Sent despatch reporting arrival at 200 mile circle. Seas heavy, barometer dropping rapidly.

0500 Xray 10/26/42 — Set all ships clocks ahead one (1) hour to zone plus ten time. Rough going all day - seas and winds of gale force.

0600 William 10/27/42 — Submerged earlier than usual for morning twilight due to moonlight condition and proximity to AKUTAN PASS. Surfaced at 0800. Contacted surface escort, YP-333, at 0915.

1317 William 10/27/42 — Arrived at Submarine Base, DUTCH HARBOR.

2. WEATHER

(a) Enroute PARAMUSHIRU; moderate seas, wind and seas from the east. Good visibility with only occasional rain squalls.

(b) East coast PARAMUSHIRU; moderate seas, wind and seas from the southeast. Visibility averaged fifteen miles.

(c) Enroute ALEUTIAN Chain; heavy seas, rain and a 25-40 knots wind for the first three days. Wind and seas initially from the southeast, then shifting to south and west. Weather was excellent after this period, with long low swells and light winds from the west. Experienced seas and winds of gale force on the 25 th and 26 th.

3. TIDAL INFORMATION

(a) Enroute PARAMUSHIRU the currents were negligible.

(b) PARAMUSHIRU, the eastern coast and ONEKOTAN KAIKYO the currents observed were in agreement with indications shown on charts and in Japan Pilot Volume 1, 1938.

(c) Enroute DUTCH HARBOR, currents were negligible.

4. NAVIGATIONAL AIDS

(a) Mountain peaks, rocks and tangents on PARAMUSHIRU viewed from the eastern waters were easily recognizable (H.O. chart 5322).

- 8 -

CONFIDENTIAL

Ps

Subject: U.S.S. S-32 - Report of Fifth War Patrol.

(b) A white light is located near the lower extremity of KURABU ZAKI (latitude 50-00-00 North, longitude 155-23-00 East). This light had no regular period and was used apparently only for certain reasons. At times it was steady, then flashing and once appeared to be signalling.

5. DESCRIPTION OF ENEMY SHIPS

Contact:	Date-Time :	Position :	Course:	Speed:	Description
No. 1	10/17/42 1328 Love	Lat. 50-25N: Lg. 156-23E.	000° T.	12	Vessel of about 6000 tons; three island, raked bow; cruiser stern; very high bow and stern, two high masts with heavy cross-trees, single stack at even height with bridge structure amidships just abaft bridge; could make out derricks housed on after mast. Believe this vessel to the raider "MANYO MARU" or very same type as shown on page 21 of "German and Italian merchantmen and Raiders in the Pacific Ocean".
No. 2	10/18/42	Lat. 50-01N.	-	0	Two large freighters at anchor in MUSASHI WAN. Tonnage 5000-6000 tons. Type similar to "HAKODATE MARU" shown on plate #98 in pamphlet "Recognition of Japanese Merchantmen".
No. 3	10/19/42 1303 Love	Lat. 50-00N. Lg. 158-25E	095°T. and 125°T.	15	Destroyer of the "SHIGURE" class.

6. AIRCRAFT SIGHTED

Contact:	Date-Time :	Type :	Position :	Course:	Altitude ;	Remarks
No. 1	10/9/42 0709 Xray	Navy PBY	Lat. 52-15N: Lg. 167-45W.	000°T.	2000 Ft.	Exchanged recognition signals.

CONFIDENTIAL

Subject: U.S.S. S-32 - Report of Fifth War Patrol.

- -

Contact	Date-time	Type	Position	Course	Altitude	Remarks
2	10/9/42 1040 Xray	Navy PBY	Lat.52-00N. Lg.168-24W.	000°T.	1500ft.	Plane passed out of sight to westward and gave no indication of sighting us.
3.	10/11/42 0711 Xray	Army B-26	Lat.50-27N. Lg.178-14W	250°T.	1500ft.	This plane was heading directly for us and the O.O.D. was not too positive of identification at the time so we dove to escape Belive plane was Army B-26.
4.	10/11/42 1202 Xray	Navy PBY	Lt.50-23N. Lg.179-11W.	090°T	2000ft.	Plane passed out of sight to the eastward and gave no indication of sighting us.
5.	10/12/42 0815 Yoke	Navy PBY	Lt.50-38N. Lg.176-15E	270°T.	1500ft.	Exchanged recognition signals.
6.	10/23/42 0847 Yoke	Navy PBY	Lt.50-36N. Lg.177-35E	270°T	3000ft.	Plane passed out of sight to the westward and gave no indication of sighting us.
7.	10/24/42 0723 Yoke	Navy PBY	Lt.51-07N. Lg.177-23W.	270°T	1000ft.	Plane passed out of sight to the westward and gave no indication of sighting us.

- 10 -

CONFIDENTIAL

Subject: U.S.S. S-32 - Report of Fifth War Patrol.

- -

7. SUMMARY OF ATTACKS

Form report submitted to Comsubpac with original of report.

8. ENEMY A/S MEASURES

On October 19, a destroyer was sighted apparently out looking for us after our attack on the 18th in MUSASHI WAN. At this time we were less than 100 miles from attack location. We attempted to close destroyer but she finally disappeared on course 125 degrees true. It was surmised that she had left from KASHIWABARA WAN in response to our attack and was searching on a circular course from that location. No other patrolling craft was sighted.

9. None Encountered.

10. MAJOR DEFECTS EXPERIENCED

None, except for the leak in the after trim tank that occured during our fourth war patrol and was not located during our refit period.

11. COMMUNICATIONS

Radio Reception

(a) 19.8 Kcs. proved to be undesirable while we were at our maximum distance from NPG. The noise level was generally higher than the signal strength. During the hours when NPG was unreadable, NPM came in strength five.

(b) NPG on 30.6 Kcs. had the same characteristics as in (a) above, however this frequency was seldom used.

- 11 -

CONFIDENTIAL

Subject: U.S.S. S-32 - Report of Fifth War Patrol.

(c) We were unable to use 115 kcs. except for an occassional time tick.

(d) All high frequencies offered their usual dawn and evening twilight minimums but this did not hamper reception seriously. The general stability of high frequency was realized.

(e) In summation it is reasonable to assume that reception would be assured if NPM were guarded in this area.

(f) Reception from NPG was impossible during submerged operations near PARAMUSHIRU but within 200 miles from ATTU ISLAND we experienced very good reception using the loop atenna while submerged to 50 feet.

Radio Transmissions
(a) No contact was made on 16940 kcs. in spite of indications showing resonance and out put. A neon light was used to verify antenna radiation. Due to the sharpness of this frequency it was not fully expected to make a contact since there is no scheduled time for alert tuning. No signals were heard on this frequency.
(b) An attempt to make contact on 8470 kcs., a very conventional frequency for early evening transmissions, failed to bring results. This tends to indicate that very little effort is made to guard this frequency alertly.
(c) Contact was made on 4235 kcs. long after dark with NPC and NPG (NPG was utilized). We received NPG strength five but they informed us that our transmission gave them poor reception. We assume now that 3000 miles is maximum working distance for our TAR transmitter on 4235 kcs., when working conditions are normally good.

Interference
(a) All of NPG's fox schedule frequencies except 14150 kcs. were at one time or another interferred with by Japanese "chopping". In some cases the interferrence was so intense as to make that frequency useless. The shore station located at KURABU ZAKI set up an interferrence on all of NPG's fox schedule frequencies on the night of the 18th. This was the night after our attack there. Reception was possible on the high frequencies in spite of this interferrence.

Last consecutive serial sent - QUIET HARBOR.
Last consecutive serial received - ELF COVE.

12. SOUND CONDITIONS AND DENSITY LAYERS
(a) No occasions presented to enable us to determine conditions of sound, but it was assumed to be only fair.
(b) No density layers detected.

- 12 - ENCLOSURE "C"

CONFIDENTIAL Ps

Subject: U.S.S. S-32 - Report of Fifth War Patrol.

- -

13. HEALTH AND HABITABILITY

Health was excellent throughout the patrol. Only one man was placed on the sick list (two days) as a result of a severe attack of constipation. He fully recovered. Vitamin pills were administered regularly and certainly proved their value. The food seemed better than on any previous patrol in spite of a lack of fresh vegetables from the start. The new type dehydrated potatoes seem equal in flavor and desirability with fresh potatoes.

There was an abundance of reading material which is ever welcome and should never be forgotten.

The entire crew seemed in better spirit and morale was higher than ever before. Of course our patrol area and lucky results had much to do with this.

14. MILES STEAMED ENROUTE TO AND FROM STATION

(a) DUTCH HARBOR TO CAPE WRANGELL	1007
(b) CAPE WRANGELL TO HOROMUSHIRO	617
(c) EAST COAST PARAMUSHIRU	75
(d) DURABU ZAKI TO DUTCH HARBOR	1607
Total	3306

15. FUEL OIL EXPENDED

26,700 gallons (includes losses from all causes).

16. FACTORS OF ENDURANCE REMAINING

Torpedoes	Fuel	Provisions	Fresh Water	Personnel
8	2000	(14 days)	Self-Sustaining	(14 days)

17. FACTOR CAUSING END OF THIS PATROL

(a) Fuel.

(b) Orders to return by October 28, 1942.

18. REMARKS

It is very disconcerting when a shore station radio operator insists the despatch you have sent him is in error. Such happened to us twice during this patrol and entailed breaking radio silence four times unnecessarily in order to finally clear our two messages. The operator, in both cases, insisted our second and next to last group in the encoded despatch should be identical. In both these cases such was not true and we had great difficulty in convincing the operators at NPG that we wanted our despatch placed on the Fox schedule as we sent it and not as they wanted to send it. Something should be done to inform the supervisors at NPG that there are more than one type of code or cipher. The Commanding Officer desires to command the officers and crew for their actions and devotion to duty during a time when it appeared our chances were going to be rather slim.

1st copy

FF12-10/A16-3(5)/(16) SUBMARINE FORCE, PACIFIC FLEET 1d

Serial 0476
DECLASSIFIED
CONFIDENTIAL

Care of Fleet Post Office,
San Francisco, California,
April 11, 1943.

COMSUBPAC PATROL REPORT NO. 163
U.S.S. S-32 - SIXTH WAR PATROL.

From: The Commander Submarine Force, Pacific Fleet.
To : Submarine Force, Pacific Fleet.

Subject: U.S.S. S-32 (SS137) - Report of Sixth War Patrol.

Reference: (a) Comsubpac Conf. despatch 130530 of March 1943.

Enclosure: (A) Copy of Subject War Patrol Report.
(B) Comtaskgroup 16.5 (CSS 45) Conf. ltr. TG16.5/A16-3
Serial 032 of March 25, 1943.

1. The sixth war patrol of the U.S.S. S-32 was carried out in an aggressive and successful manner. In spite of continued stormy, Arctic weather, the S-32 covered the area thoroughly and efficiently.

2. It is gratifying to note the improved performance of the Sugar-class submarines as the installation of the latest type war-time alterations are effected. The decided advantages of the SJ radar and the fathometer are particularly noted in this patrol; both were used efficiently in navigating and the former in making successful torpedo attacks.

3. The Commander Submarine Force, Pacific Fleet, congratulates the Commanding Officer, officers and crew of the S-32 for its successful and aggressive war patrol.

4. In accordance with reference (a), the Commander Task Force Sixteen is requested to credit the S-32 with the damage inflicted on the enemy as stated in paragraph 6 of enclosure (B).

J. H. BROWN, Jr.,
Acting.

DISTRIBUTION:
(1M-43)
List III, SS
Special:
P1(5), EN3(5), Z1(5),
Comsublant (2), X3(1),
Comsubsowespac (2),
Subschool, NL (2),
Comtaskfor 72 (2),
Comsubron 50 (2)
Comsopac (2),
Cinclant (2),
Comtaskfor 16 (1).

FILMED
48630

E. R. SWINBURNE,
Flag Secretary.

MAY 1 1943
80854

CONFIDENTIAL Jk

U.S.S. S-32 -- Report of Six War Patrol.

Period From: February 6, 1943 to March 20, 1943.

OPERATION ORDER: Commander Task Group Eight Point Five Operation Order 8-43.

PROLOGUE:

Arrived DUTCH HARBOR from FIFTH WAR PATROL at 1317 WILLIAM on October 27, 1942. Made minor repairs, fueled and prepared for trip to San Diego in accordance with Squadron Schedule. During battery equalizing charge the starboard main motor developed full ground. Investigation showed main motor armature grounded due to commutator bars coming loose and being thrown out of place. Starboard main motor placed out of commission and preparations made with DesBase, San Diego, for renewal upon arrival.

Departed DUTCH HARBOR at 1000 WILLIAM, November 1, 1942 enroute San Diego, California. Arrived San Diego at 1430 TARE on November 11, 1942.

Commenced overhaul upon arrival DesBase, San Diego. Remained under overhaul until December 19, 1942. Conducted post overhaul runs during 21 - 25 December 1942.

During overhaul the following major work, repairs and alterations were completed:

1. Docked and undocked.
2. Installed Kleinschmidt vapor-compressor still.
3. Installed JK Radar.
4. Installed fathometer, Model WCA-1.
5. Installed JK-QC (keel mounted).
6. Main engine overhaul.
7. Starboard main motor armature renewed.
8. C. & R. air compressor overhauled.

Commenced working with West Coast Sound School on December 28, 1942. Completed work with Sound School on January 26, 1943.

Re-docked between January 27 and February 1, 1943 to check and alter stern plane spool bearing securing bolts and to complete main ballast tank grease work.

During February 2 - 5 refueled; ship was wiped; trained and prepared for sea.

During the work with Sound School one hour was granted in the late afternoon for torpedo practice approaches and firings. This period was utilized to fire ten "Z-2" practices and one (1)

CONFIDENTIAL Jk

Subject: U.S.S. S-32 - Report of Sixth War Patrol.

- -

modified night practice using radar plot (daylight run actually). It is believed this opportunity was invaluable but the lack of night work is regretted.

Departed San Diego at 0900 TARE February 6, 1943.

1. NARRATIVE

February 6, 1943 0900 TARE	Departed San Diego, California for DUTCH HARBOR in accordance Commander Task Unit Eight Point Five Point One Operation Order 1-43. Surface escort SC-645 in company.
1126 TARE	Submerged for trim check and training, surfacing at 1143. Continued course and speed.
February 7, 1943 1112 TARE	Went to battle stations surface and fired ten (10) rounds target ammunition from deck gun for training. At 1200 released surface escort (SC-645).
1235 TARE	Master gyro went out. Our magnetic compass unreliable since wiping so commenced steering by sun and stars. Started repairs to gyro.
February 8, 1943 1658 TARE	Sighted Army bomber bearing 000°(T) distance 3 miles. Exchanged recognition signals satisfactorily.
February 10, 1943 0300 UNCLE	Gyro repairs finally completed and resumed steering by gyro.
February 13, 1943 1805 VICTOR	Submerged for training and evening twilight, surfacing at 1821.
February 18, 1943 0622 WILLIAM	Radar picked up object bearing 000 degrees true - heavy fog - visibility 400 yards. Bearing changed slowly aft; range closed to 400 yards before finally sighting steady white light. Made out dim outline of merchant ship (presumably Russian since Comalsec position report of friendly ships located several vessels near us south of UNIMAK PASS). Lost vessel in fog; radar tracked her out to 10,000 yards.

CONFIDENTIAL Jk

Subject: U.S.S. S-32 - Report of Sixth War Patrol.

- -

By combining the use of radar, fathometer and radio direction finder (portable) we navigated UNIMAK PASS in dense fog without sighting land. At 0707 sighted SCOTCH CAP LIGHT momentarily and bearing checked satisfactorily.

0741 WILLIAM Sighted SCOTCH CAP and surrounding land for first time. Set course 290° (T) to clear islands to port. At this time the electric steering motor commenced smoking; shifted to hand steering. Casualty due to the field coil holding bolts breaking and allowing the coil to drop on top the armature. Repairs must be made at DUTCH because a spare armature is necessary.

Heavy storm suddenly broke and mountainous seas from 320° (T) soon built up. Visibility between 500 yards and 5 miles, varying.

1611 WILLIAM Moored at Submarine Base, DUTCH HARBOR, ALASKA.

Commenced minor repairs and checking; fueled and made preparations for sea on 24 February 1943. Installed re-ligned deck gun barrel.

February 25, 1943

1000 WILLIAM Departed DUTCH HARBOR for patrol area assigned in accordance with Commander Task Group Eight Point Five Operation Order 8-43. No air coverage but surface escort by YP-57.

1140 WILLIAM Submerged for trim check. Went deep for tightness check. Satisfactory. Surfaced at 1202 and fired five (5) rounds service ammunition at floating target dropped by escort vessel. This was necessary to check ballistics on newly installed gun barrel.

1320 WILLIAM Released surface escort vessel.

1743 WILLIAM Sighted BOGOSLOF ISLAND bearing 280 degrees true, and at 1920 WILLIAM passed the islands abeam to starboard distance 4 miles.

Seas began picking up and a violent storm soon broke. The wind and seas were from our port quarter, pooping us easily. Did not make evening and morning twilight dives for considered state of seas making these dives unnecessary.

CONFIDENTIAL Jk

Subject: U.S.S. S-32 - Report of Sixth War Patrol.

February 26, 1943 1201 WILLIAM	Sighted Navy PBY bearing 135 degrees true distance 2 miles. The plane, although passing within 1000 yards made no apparent signs of sighting us. We attempted to exchange recognition signals without results. The plane disappeared in the haze bearing 270° T.
1500 WILLIAM	Set ships clocks back one hour to zone plus eleven time (XRay).
	Storm increasing in intensity and wind and seas shifting to the south. During the night we rolled as much as 65 degrees to the starboard. Really tough going.
February 27, 1943 0850 XRAY	Forced to slow to one engine to prevent flooding control room for it is impossible to run on main induction only - the entire ship is under water at times, and the seas have shifted nearer the bow. At 1815 the seas started abating somewhat and we went ahead on both engines at 2/3 speed again.
2000 XRAY	Radar out of commission - attempting repairs.
February 28, 1943 0705 XRAY	Submerged for twilight and training. Seas have smoothed out considerably. Surfaced at 0811.
1100 XRAY	Set all ships clocks back one hour to zone plus twelve time (YOKE).
1134 YOKE	Sighted plane dead ahead distance 10,000 yards headed directly toward us. Dive immediately. O.O.D. stated he believed plane to be a PBY but was taking no chances since he appeared to be less than 50 feet above the water headed right at us. Went to 100 feet, changed course to 180 degrees true for 20 minutes. Came up to periscope depth for a look. No plane in sight. We have developed a loud screeching noise in starboard shaft. By process of elimination this noise was located somewhere between engine clutch and tail clutch. Decided it was a newly installed main motor wiper ring. Remained submerged to remove this ring and make noise tests. After removal of wiper ring the noise disappeared and at

CONFIDENTIAL Jk

Subject: U.S.S. S-32 - Report of Sixth War Patrol.

- -

1318 YOKE	Surfaced and resumed course and speed. Still unable to find trouble in the radar. The transmitter appears O.K. but cannot work on the receiver until we are submerged and calm. The conning tower ladder must be removed in order to clear gear sufficiently to pull and handle heavy radar receiver units. Only in this manner can we make a thorough check to effect repairs. We intend to do this tomorrow, after we enter our patrol area and are conducting a patrol submerged. Seas and wind abated somewhat. We still have no exact idea where we are. I intend to head towards the SEMICHI - ATTU line and commence patrol along this line approaching SARANA BAY. Any land will be a welcome sight. Our fathometer does not give any results in deep water while we are rolling heavily. Radar still out of commission.
March 1, 1943 0830 YOKE	Submerged and commenced our submerged patrol, having figured we entered our assigned area about 0300 YOKE.
1052 YOKE	Sighted land bearing 224 degrees true but unable to identify until at 1130 YOKE finally obtained a good fix on ALAID and the other two islands in the SEMICHI group. Our fathometer works exceedingly well while submerged. Readings over 2000 fathoms with a strong return signal are consistent. Changed our course to approach SARANA BAY but our time left will not allow us to reach there today. Surfaced at
1850 YOKE	Charged batteries and patrolled at one engine speed on a northerly course across enemy possible tracks. Radar is still out of commission but much progress towards repairs has been made. Changed course during the night to head towards HOLTZ BAY.
March 2, 1943 0620 YOKE	Submerged and headed south to make a landfall. At 1350 YOKE sighted land dead ahead and finally identified it as STELLER COVE. Had much difficulty in identifying our position; mainly due to heavy mist and fog obscuring all land above about 500 feet and the fact that this is our first time along this coast line. By the time we definitely fixed our

CONFIDENTIAL

Jk

Subject: U.S.S. S-32 - Report of Sixth War Patrol.

position it was too late to reconnoiter HOLTZ BAY, but we gave STEELER COVE a good scouting with negative results. Made record of depths on chart for future reference.

1910 YOKE

Surfaced about four (4) miles from STELLER COVE entrance and lay to while charging the batteries, It was estimated that we were in an excellent position to intercept any coastal shipping from CAPE WRANGELL to HOLTZ BAY. At 2253 YOKE went ahead 2/3 speed on one engine to patrol a north - south line across enemy lanes. Plan to reconnoiter HOLTZ BAY tomorrow. Our radar is finally repaired sufficiently to get fair results. One more work day submerged and it should be fully repaired.

March 3, 1943.
0633 YOKE

Submerged and proceeded towards HOLTZ BAY. The weather got bad during early morning and a good storm is indicated. A fog set in and this combined with heavy seas (poor periscope depth control) dictates a cautious shoreline approach. Our fathometer is priceless as far as we are concerned. Without it, it would be sheer folly to approach these bays as we are and plan to do. Finally worked our way to within 1½ miles from HOLTZ BAY. The seas are enormous and the wind is creating a "dust storm" over the water so finally decided to get out and northwest by at least five miles. Unable to see clearly into either arm of the bay. At 90 feet we roll 15 degrees to each side and at periscope depth we run a high rate battery discharge; no radio reception submerged over the loop (even when we broach) so consider this is no day for reconnaisance.

1900 YOKE

Surfaced in full gale - forced to accept a course of 070 degrees true at 1/3 speed one engine to ride out gale while charging battery.

2010 YOKE

Received CTG 8.5 "HOONAH". Will attempt to be in good position to carry out orders in the morning. The gale may prevent such.

2208 YOKE

Received CTG 8.5 "ISLETA POINT". The gale shows no evidence of subsiding. During the night we took at least three rolls to starboard for 65 degrees.

ENCLOSURE (A)

CONFIDENTIAL

Jk

Subject: U.S.S. S-32 - Report of Sixth War Patrol.

- -

March 4, 1943
0615 YOKE — Submerged and took a course to head us for SARANA BAY but at 1830 YOKE we found out the gale had blown us west as much as the current had set us east so we were just about 4 miles north of ALAID ISLAND. At any rate a north - south line patrol on the surface tonight will cover tracks according CTG 8.5 "HOONAH".

1920 YOKE — Surfaced and commenced patrol and battery charge.

0815 YOKE — Submerged and headed towards the SEMICHIS. Patrolled from these islands on a diagonal across possible tracks of enemy submarine. The weather is excellent and visibility near maximim. We are able to conduct practically a constant periscope patrol. We also obtained more fathometer readings for record.

1003 YOKE — Sighted plane over ALAID on easterly course. Believe plane to be Army B-24 (weather plane). Obtained periscope photos of ALAID.

March 5, 1943
1500 YOKE — Noticed the trim getting heavy forward and after investigating discovered the sound well and H.P. air bottle well in torpedo room a bout 60 percent flooded. T he sound well is inspected twice daily, at 0800 and 2000. This morning's inspection showed it dry. The wells were pumped and a large leak around JK - QC shaft discovered where the screw type packing gland nut had backed out of position and thus allowed packing to be forced up and out. Quite a sizeable stream of water was pouring in. Work was immediately started to correct casualty and after 13 hours - success. (See remarks under machinery derangements).

1918 YOKE — Surfaced - charged battery and patrolled on a north-south line across possible enemy routes. Our Keel - mounted sound gear is inoperative due to flooding around electrical units. We hope to have it functioning by morning. The radar is now working perfectly.

March 6, 1943
0610 YOKE — Submerged and lay course to SARANA BAY. Made reconnaissance of this bay (negative results) and decided to patrol tonight off CHICHAGOF HARBOR hoping to intercept something - expecially the Jap submarine. Heard many strange noises - "YEHOODI" - in SARANA BAY.

-7-

ENCLOSURE (A)

CONFIDENTIAL

Ww

Subject: U.S.S. S-32 - Report of Sixth War Patrol.

- -

March 6, 1943 (Continued)

1923 YOKE — Surfaced and patrolled just off CHICHAGOF and HOLTZ BAY entrances and charged battery.

2229 YOKE — The O.O.D. sighted a white light in HOLTZ BAY apparently signalling. Proceeded immediately towards light and got into the entrance of HOLTZ BAY before stopping. Made out two white lights, one in each arm of the Bay. Visibility was from very good to bad. Heavy snow fell occassionally. Radar worked perfectly but we could not determine any moving targets. Finally at

2340 YOKE — We proceeded out of harbor and patrolled on a north - south line just off entrance; hoping that the signalling was for an expected arrival or departure. We were unlucky for nothing further happened. Do not believe any shipping could have avoided us during this time for the radar and visibility combination surely would have allowed detection. Tomorrow I will get a good look inside to make sure nothing did get by us into the bay. After this reconnaissance I will return to my patrol accordance task group commanders orders. This deviation, under the circumstances, I feel is absolutely warranted.

There is one interesting feature about the small islands off the north-west entrance to CHICHAGOF HARBOR and that is we found [illegible] ISLAND to appear exactly like a large submarine except the bow is slightly larger than ordinary. This is true when viewed from a bearing about 320 degrees from the island. It gave us quite a start and the idea we really had something when we approached HOLTZ BAY tonight.

March 7, 1943

0555 YOKE — Submerged and conducted a careful reconnaissance of HOLTZ BAY. Took several periscope photos. Examined CHICHAGOF HARBOR and proceeded down the coast into SARANA BAY. All information negative.

1210 YOKE — Sound reported two dull explosions - far away. Nothing could be seen through periscope.

1930 YOKE — Surfaced after thoroughly scouting SARANA BAY, and commenced a surface patrol, while charging battery, on a north - south line just north of SARANA BAY. Looks like another storm forming in the southeast. Wind and seas picking up.

ENCLOSURE (A)

CONFIDENTIAL Ww

Subject: U.S.S. S-32 - Report of Sixth War Patrol.

- -

March 7, 1943 (Continued)

2255 YOKE Received CTG 8.5 "KANE ISLANDS" directing us to conduct close reconnaissance of HOLTZ BAY, CHICHAGOF HARBOR and SARANA BAY. No further information concerning his "HOONAH".

Seas and wind still picking up with a full gale in view. The radar cuts out (motor generator) every time we take a heavy roll to starboard. Some adjustment must be wrong or the brush rigging shifts to give overload when rolling. T he wind is now at about 40 knots and visibility bad.

March 8, 1943

0608 YOKE Submerged - took course to enter SARANA BAY. Visibility only about 1000 yards but at times open up sufficiently to see land. Periscope depth control is again almost impossible without a high rate discharge. In spite of the weather we are able, with aid of fathometer, to reconnoiter SARANA BAY and just off the entrances of CHICHAGOF HARBOR and HOLTZ BAY. No evidence of enemy shipping.

1903 YOKE Surfaced again in a gale and forced to accept a course of 290 degrees true and speed to prevent flooding control room. Most of the time riding with upper conning tower hatch closed while charging on one engine and going ahead 2/3 on the other.

The radar gave excellent results in these heavy seas getting good "pips" at 24,000 yards on mountains.

2300 YOKE Changed course to 110 degrees true and slowed to 1/3 on one engine. No evidence of the gale breaking up and all hands, as well as the ship, taking a severe beating.

The keel-mounted sound gear out of commission as a result of the cable leads getting chewed up when caught in the gearing of the limit switches. Poor installation caused this; we have constantly tried to improve the condition. We finally repaired the cables and readjusted the limit switch for two complete turns only instead of two and one half. This may prevent the cable kind that forces cable near limit switch gear.

- 9 - ENCLOSURE (A)

CONFIDENTIAL Jk

Subject: U.S.S. S-32 - Report of Sixth War Patrol.

- -

March 9, 1943

0608 YOKE Submerged and headed toward what we thought would be SARANA BAY but at

1000 YOKE Obtained fix on ALAID and showed us only about 30 miles out of position. This means the current during the night had a set of 098 degrees true and drift of 2.2 knots - exactly 170 degrees to the right of the direction of sea and wind. More gray hairs and the only thing that prevents the few remaining hairs to turn gray is the radar - fathometer factor.

1035 YOKE Altered course to lead us toward SARANA BAY. It is another day of terrible periscope depth control. Torpedo fire in this type sea, predominent in this area now, would surely be a waste of material.

1400 YOKE Seas moderating so plan to surface just off the N.E. point of CHICHAGOF HARBOR.

1915 YOKE Surfaced. Went ahead 2/3 speed on one engine patrolling and charging the battery on the other.

2012 YOKE Sighted steady white light (off the surface) in HOLTZ BAY. This may be a light of a ship entering or leaving the bay.

2014 YOKE Sighted a dark object, that may be a ship, bearing 305 degrees true range about 6000 yards. (Contact # 1) Went to battle stations - secured battery charge - various courses and speeds conducting a night surface attack. Trained radar on ship and got a range of 4250 yards. Weather conditions: sea and wind moderate; visibility fair in northern semi-circle. Toward land it is very dark and murky with low dark clouds. Am apprehensive about the white light (not now showing) for it may be another ship approaching from dark background and it would have us well outlined in the clear sector.

Continued surface approach. Our target seemed to be milling around keeping bare steerageway probably making a rendezvous. The silhouette later proved very much like that of the "UN #1" (new DD) shown in the ONI weekly Vol. II, No. 2 dated January 13, 1943, but I don't think she was that long unless she was never broadside to. Her single snaked stack is exactly as that shown. She is certainly a destroyer or a large CM. The nearest

CONFIDENTIAL

Jk

Subject: U.S.S. S-32 - Report of Sixth War Patrol.

- -

CM silhouette is the one shown in ONI 14, Page 155, the 1200 ton CM-9 SHIMUSHU CLASS. We did not have sufficient time to study details of his silhouette but the snaked single stack stood out strongly. Made ready all tubes at 2030 YOKE. Had radar operator training around periodically to search for any other ships. Radar operator got a "pip" bearing 213 degrees relative range 5000 yards but the word received on the bridge was 13 relative and a thorough search on this bearing revealed only a clear horizon. I instructed radar operator to then stay on our target for we were soon to fire. This of course was my big mistake but I thought nothing was within range except our target. Later developments prove that radar had picked up the ship that depth charged us after attack.

2039 YOKE The destroyer changed course to her left and headed directly at us. This was a bad few seconds but she finally swung further left and gave me a beautiful starboard track with very little headway. So at

2042 YOKE Fired four torpedoes (radar range 700 yards) at intervals of 20 - 15 - 20 seconds. (Attack #1) The target gave no indications of having sighted us even during the firing. Just as I ordered "Fire 4" there was a terrific explosion felt and heard by all hands and we were soon to find out it was not a depth charge. The time interval for number two torpedo run was perfect for a hit. At this time we were on our way down - bridge cleared except for the O.O.D and myself.

The O.O.D. saw a plume of spray well inside the stern of the DD at the time of the explosion; as I fired four and cleared the bridge. I was still worried about another vessel because of the light we sighted. Visibility towards HOLTZ BAY was no more than 800 yards. I had previously made up my mind to fire and dive unless everything looked clearer than it did. One lookout, as he cleared the bridge insists he saw a second ship but failed to say anything at the time. I guess his tongue was tied by all the activity.

As we passed by 55 feet in the fastest dive we ever made the first of a string of 3 depth charges exploded - close - and the torpedo room personnel reported a ship as having passed directly overhead

- 11 - ENCLOSURE (A)

from port to starboard. At this time we were changing course to the left, away from target and our heading was about 300 degrees.

This confirms my fears that another ship was coming out of the bay while we made our approach, and was unseen by us. Later confirmed by radar operator. She undoubtedly saw us and attempted to ram, luckily we got under and the best she could do was a working over with depth charges, which she did. Went to 180 feet, completed rig for depth charge and took evasive action. After we dove the initial bearing by sound prior attack on us was 290 degrees relative. DD did not echo-range but seemed to have good listening gear. She would only stop for about 2 seconds to get a bearing and then speed up. Our second attack by depth charges came 12 minutes later and was a good close pattern of 4 a little astern and on each quarter. Interval 5 - 10 - 12 seconds and most certainly laid, using throwers. All charges seemed to be set shallower than we were riding.

2125 YOKE — Can now only hear his screws faintly and intermittently and hope he has gone back to assist his sister ship. The 5th patrol report of the USS S-31 reports a SHIMUSHU type CM at MUSASHI WAN and this leads me to believe that our target may have been this vessel instead of a destroyer. The only thing that makes me hesitate is the appearance of the "UN #1" type single funnel. Conducted torpedo reload. At

2242 YOKE — Surfaced. Our battery very low and we had better get clear and charge as quickly as possible. Upon surfacing saw a large "orange - white " glow, undoubtedly from a huge fire, bearing 35 degrees true. This plots exactly where our scene of action was and we are now convinced more than ever of one good hit. Nothing else in sight so commenced battery charge immediately. Inspection for damage shows: "SJ" radar mast packing gland leaking very badly; cork and paint knocked off throughout ship and the port shaft noisy with a noticeable vibration not heretofore [illegible]. Engine room soft patch slight leakage. Stern tube packing compressed so glands had to be taken up considerably. Number 1 periscope packing leaking badly and unable to tighted sufficiently to stop

CONFIDENTIAL

Jk

Subject: U.S.S. S-32 - Report of Sixth War Patrol.

- -

leak completely. The seams or rivets of main lub oil tank opened up allowing fuel oil in #9 to enter main lub oil tank. No further damage found. The conning tower had about 20 gallons of water in it due to radar gland leak.

2321 YOKE — Heard distant underwater explosion, and at 0025 heard two more in rapid succession.

March 10, 1943
0315 YOKE — Charge completed. Continued surface patrol at 2/3 speed on one engine.

0550 YOKE — Submerged and conducted reconnaissance of HOLTZ BAY, CHICHAGOF HARBOR and SARANA BAY. Visibility excellent except for haze well inside harbors. No enemy acitivities noted. Heard dull explosions at the following times today: 0845 - 1420 - 1547.

1919 YOKE — Surfaced in heavy seas and again forced to accept best course and speed to ride out storm while charging battery.

March 11, 1943
0604 YOKE — Submerged. Made close reconnaissance of HOLTZ BAY and CHICHAGOF HARBOR with negative results. Seas calmed down during the day and we were able to get good, long clear looks into harbors.

March 12, 1943
0900 YOKE — Sighted plane bearing 280 degrees true distance 8 miles - appeared to be Army B-24, but positive identification uncertain. Patrolled on a north - south line out from HOLTZ BAY during the night. Conducted very close and careful reconnaissance of HOLTZ BAY and CHICHAGOF HARBOR. Visibility excellent and seas ideal. Took periscope photographs of harbors. No enemy activity noted. Watered battery. Surface patrol during night on a north - south line out from HOLTZ BAY.

March 13, 1943
0555 YOKE — Submerged and conducted another close reconnaissance of bays and harbors. Took more periscope photos.

1935 YOKE — Surfaced. Commenced surface night patrol while charging battery on a north - south line out of HOLTZ BAY.

ENCLOSURE (A)

CONFIDENTIAL Jk

Subject: U.S.S. S-32 - Report of Sixth War Patrol.

- -

2052 YOKE Ensign J.V. Delladonna (Eagle Eye John) sighted a Jap submarine, I121 or I52 class, bearing [illegible] degrees true range about 3700 yards. (Contact #2) Weather conditions were as follows: [illegible] overcast with half moon behind clouds aiding in visibility. Seas fairly rough from 200 degrees true. We were again favored with a darker background astern. Our position at this time was 17 miles north of HOLTZ BAY. Went back to battle stations immediately - shifted to motors and [illegible] commenced night surface approach. The Jap submarine appeared to be lying to on a heading of 305 degrees true charging battery for there was no relative movement and his engines were smoking heavily. This exhaust smoke is what attracted the attention of officer first sighting submarine. The swells would raise and lower him to permit us to see his deck at one time and then only his conning tower.

Assumed we were still undetected; closing range rapidly when at a range of 2500 yards his engines stopped smoking and I thought he was preparing to dive. It was shoot now or never for my torpedoes were set at 4 feet. At

2059 YOKE Fired #1 followed ten seconds later by #2. (Attack #2) The first torpedo fired ahead (in case he was getting headway) and the second fired at his conning tower. Went ahead full speed and changed course rapidly to the right and at

2100½ YOKE Dove. As we passed 50 feet in a very fast dive there was one (1) loud torpedo explosion. The tracks of both torpedoes were observed, prior diving, heading true. The best time check gives 2 minutes and 40 seconds after firing the first torpedo until the torpedo explosion was heard by all hands. We slowed immediately to dead slow [illegible] and tried to pick up his screws by sound. At no time previous to firing of after torpedo explosion was sound able to hear propeller noises. We remained submerged at 100 feet attempting to pick up any identifiable sounds; none heard. At

2120 YOKE Came to periscope depth - visibility prevented seeing anything farther than several hundred yards so at

ENCLOSURE (A)

Subject: U.S.S. S-32 - Report of Sixth War Patrol.

- -

2130 YOKE — Surfaced in slightly poorer visibility conditions than before - nothing in sight - radar results negative. Proceeded with surface patrol and battery charge. Rain and snow soon set in heavily wind and seas increasing. We are all certain that we have destroyed one Japanese submarine. This is the second time that Ensign J.J. Dellad[illegible], U.S. N.R. has picked up an enemy by sight at night before radar contact. Our radar training must improve. Completed torpedo reload and checks on tubes #3 and #4 since they were flooded. Conditions satisfactory.

March 14, 1943
0117 YOKE — Radar operator reported target bearing 135 degrees relative range 1250 yards. Went to battle stations. Unable to pick up object by sight. radar reporting bearings from 035 relative [illegible] to the right to 200 relative with ranges varying from 450 yards to 1000 yards. Finally decided it was "pips" from waves (the seas had increased a lot) combined with a case of "nerves" of the operator. It was also snowing and raining with the wind about 25 knots from due South.

0145 YOKE — Secured from battle stations and resumed surface patrol and battery charge.

0545 YOKE — Submerged and commenced patrol towards HOLTZ BAY. Attempted to allow for previously encountered currents and headed to westward of HOLTZ BAY. When land was finally sighted we found our D.R. within four miles being correct. The currents in this area are certainly non-conformists. There has been a heavy gale blowing all day with accompanying poor visibility and rugged periscope depth control. Unable to reconnoiter HOLTZ BAY today.

1945 YOKE — Surfaced in another heavy gale and forced to accept best course and speed patrolling on surface while charging battery.

March 15, 1943
0700 YOKE — Gale subsiding sufficiently to change course to 080 degrees true and get in a good position for submerged patrol today.

- -

0533 YOKE — Submerged and commenced patrol towards HOLTZ BAY. When position was fixed changed course

1350 YOKE — To head across entrance to HOLTZ BAY.

1430 YOKE — Sound reported screw noises mixed in with "YEHOODI" bearing 185 degrees true, RPM count 140. Periscope observations negative.

1700 YOKE — Sound heard noises resembling "pinging" but there was no reverberation acquainted with echo-ranging. It could be a fathometer with a broader beam than our type.

1713 YOKE — Sound suddenly heard screws bearing 325 degrees true. Periscope observation revealed Japanese I-1 class submarine (Contact #3) estimated range 6000 yards, bearing 318 degrees true on course 200 degrees true. First speed count 190 RPM and three minutes later 240 RPM. Estimated speed at 13 knots. Weather conditions perfect for periscope approach. Bright sun; white caps, and moderate sea. Battle stations and commenced approach. Went ahead full to close track and came to course 220 degrees true. Made tubes ready for firing. Sub changed course to 140 degrees true and this then gave me about 100 degree port track angle. I saw it was to be a fairly long range shot in order to get a favorable track angle; estimated torpedo run was 2500 yards. We were rapidly closing the beach and certainly couldn't proceed on a southerly course too long. There were 2 white numerals or letter and numeral painted high up on his conning tower. At

1727 YOKE — Fired a 3 torpedo spread (Attack #3) using zero gyro angles spread about 70% target length. Commenced changing course to the right to north to clear beach and area. Personnel in the torpedo room heard a muffled report about 2½ minutes after firing but no explosions were heard by me or control party.

When steadied on course north I slowed and observed enemy for evidence of a hit. The submarine bore 210 degrees true and a tremendous plume of dark, greenish-gray smoke was pouring toward the sky above his conning tower. The mass of smoke appeared to be at least 200 feet in the air. I let all officers and control room personnel observe this picture. The sub was still making 240 RPM - there was no change in speed until he finally stopped. His bearing varied five degrees during this 6 minute observation period and the smoke continued billowing toward the sky with a snow covered mountain for a perfect background. Took one periscope photo. His course was heading him toward nearest beach head and he was changing course erratically.

1736 YOKE Submarine suddenly disappeared from view and at this instant sound reported screws had stopped. Except for one instant, his conning tower was all I had in view during post firing observation.

I cannot explain the failure to hear any loud explosion and still observe the submarine billowing such an enormous plume of smoke for he was clearly in plenty of trouble and apparently trying to beach himself. I also find it hard to believe that a submarine can withstand a torpedo hit so long. I am frankly quite puzzled.

2005 YOKE Surfaced and commenced patrol on one engine while charging on the other.

2111 YOKE The O.O.D. sighted a bright white light bearing 275 degrees true. Went ahead on both engines to investigate; course 275. Battle stations. The position of this light was estimated 15 miles north of RED HEAD. It disappeared about one second before I reached the bridge. Continued course until we thought we could surely see a ship had one been there not heading away at high speed. Radar gave no contacts except land to port. At

2200 YOKE Secured battle stations - continued one engine patrol and battery charge. Changed course to North. The weather was perfect for a night periscope attack; bright half moon; cleak skies and horizon. This light may have been from another submarine and a trap to lure us in to his range. Sent a message to CTF 16 and CTG 16.5 making full report.

Subject: U.S.S. S-32 - Report of Sixth War Patrol.

March 16, 1943 0535 YOKE	Submerged and commenced patrol towards HOLTZ BAY. Have to leave area tonight according to OP Order 8-43. Foggy and hazy over ATTU. Approached to within 5 miles.
1951 YOKE	Surfaced. Commenced patrol on course 040 degrees true enroute point "George" and thence along track enroute DUTCH HARBOR. Bright moon, clear skies, calm seas and wind 10 knots.
March 17, 1943 0230 YOKE	Left patrol area.
0400 YOKE	Arrived point "George" and changed course to 090 degrees true. At
0540 YOKE	Submerged for twilight, and at
0704 YOKE	Surfaced - continued course and speed.
0810 YOKE	Sighted plane bearing 180 degrees true distance six miles, course west. Appeared to be PBY but unable to certainly distinguish from "MAVIS" at presented angle. Dove but unable to see plane through periscope.
0817 YOKE	Surfaced. Commenced zig zag plan 94 percent base course. Visibility maximum and seas calm. Made evening twilight dive.
March 18, 1943	Submerged for morning and evening twilight. Continued zig zag plan. Seas moderate; overcast but visibility very good. Changed time to Zone Plus 11(XRAY).
March 19, 1943	Submerged for morning and evening twilight. Continued zig zag plan. Seas moderate. Changed time to Zone Plus 10 (WILLIAM).
March 20, 1943. 0530 WILLIAM	Exchanged recognition signals with surface escort (YP 57).
0930 WILLIAM	Arrived Submarine Base, DUTCH HARBOR.

CONFIDENTIAL

Subject: U.S.S. S-32 - Report of Sixth War Patrol.

- -

2. WEATHER:

February 25 - 28, 1943. Enroute Dutch Harbor, to Attu Island.

Sky was generally overcast both day and night. Very few star fixes were obtained, three to be exact. However, at intervals during day sun lines made possible a fairly accurate fix almost every day. Rain and mist reduced visibility considerably. Seas were rough and wind of strong intensity during most of passage to Attu.

March 1 - 16, 1943. On station in vicinity of Attu.

Visibility during about 50 percent of this period was very poor, due to mist, snow, and rain. Seas were alternately very rough, accompanied by high winds, and smooth, neither state lasting more than two days. Generally, the weather was very changeable. Wind and seas generally were from a southerly direction varying from southeast to southwest. Waves encountered at times were 30 to 40 feet high, and winds up to about 45 knots. All fixes were obtained by piloting and not star fixes.

March 17 - 20, 1943. Enroute Attu Area to Dutch Harbor.

Wind and seas were moderate and weather generally good to within 100 miles of Dutch Harbor, when wind picked up to about 30 knots. An easterly current of about .5 knot was encountered to within 100 miles of Dutch Harbor. Star and sun fixes were obtained.

3. TIDAL INFORMATION:

In the Attu Area the currents encountered are consistently southeast no matter what the direction of wind and seas. Currents vary in their drift from as low as .2 knot to as high as 1.9 knots, set being always easterly and predominently southeast. A definate current of one knot in a southeast direction was encountered 4 miles off Chichagof Harbor and Holtz Bay.

4. NAVIGATIONAL AIDS:

Charts containing aerial photos, soundings, and geography of land were very useful, but could and should be improved upon. It is suggested that aerial photos be taken from a very low altitude so as to give a close approximation of a submarines view. The chart showing soundings did not show contour of land or mountains. It is also suggested that large area charts of that area be compiled showing the topography of the islands, all available soundings, and views as shown in View Chart of Attu Island.

ENCLOSURE (A)

CONFIDENTIAL

Subject: U.S.S. S-32 - Report of Sixth War Patrol.

4. NAVIGATIONAL AIDS (Cont'd)

Also Chart HO Misc. 10-253-1 and USC & GS Chart 9102 show Attu Island in latitudes differing by four miles, with different northern-most points of the Island itself. Alaid Island, of the Semichi group is shown one mile south of actual position.

5. DESCRIPTION OF ENEMY SHIPS:

Contact	Date Time	Position	Course	Speed	Description
1.	3-9-43	Lat. 53-03 N.	Lying to or Steerway on station	0-?	Japanese DD of the "UN #1" class as shown in the ONI Weekly Vol. II No. 2 dated Jan. 13, 1943 or a new type (similar to WSHIMUSH class. It appeared mixture of the two during the short ti observed prior firi The single snaked stack was predominat
2.	3-13-43 2052 Y	Lat. 53-14 N. Long. 173-15 E.	Lying to charging battery	0	Japanese Submarine I-121 or I-52 Class.
3.	3-15-43 1713 Y	Lat. 52-54 N. Long. 173-13 E.	200°	13 K.	Japanese Submarine I-1 Class.

6. AIRCRAFT SIGHTED:

Contact	Date Time	Type	Position	Course	Alitude	Remarks
1.	2-28-43 1201 W.	PBY	Lat. 54° 00' N. Long. 172° 00' W.	270°	1000'	Apparentl did not s us. No exchange of signals.

ENCLOSURE (A)

CONFIDENTIAL

Ww

Subject: U.S.S. S-32 - Report of Sixth War Patrol.

6. AIRCRAFT SIGHTED: (Cont'd).

Contact	Date Time	Type	Position	Course	Altitude	Remarks
2.	2-28-43 1134 Y.	PBY	Lat. 53° 40' N: Long. 177°30'E:	090°	100'	Dove. Out of sight when surfacing. No signals.
3.	3-5-43 1003 Y.	B-24	Lat. 52° 45'N Long. 174°00'E:	090°	2000'	Plane over ALAIN Isl. Pribably Army weather plane.
4.	3-12-43 0900 Y	B-24	Lat. 53° 00'N. Long. 173°00'E.	270°	4000'	Probably Army weather plane.
5.	3-17-43 0810 Y	PBY	Lat. 54° 00' N Long. 175°50' E:	270°	1000'	Dove - Plane did not see us.
6.	3-17-43 0817 Y	PBY	Lat. 54° 10' N Long 175° 52'E	090°	1000'	May be same as #5 returning on reverse course.

7. SUMMARY OF ATTACKS:

Attack	#1	#2	#3
Date	3-9-43	3-13-43	3-15-43
Location (Lat.)	53° 03' N.	53° 14' N.	52° 54' N.
(Long.)	173° 15' E.	173° 15' E.	173° 13' E.
Torpedoes fired on each attack	4	2	3
Hits	1	1	1
Number sunk (tonnage)	-	-	1 - 1200
Number damaged or probably sunk	1 - 1500	1 - 1400	
Type of target	DD or CM	SS	SS
Range 1500 yards or less	700	-	-
Range more than 1500 yards	-	2500	2500
Periscope depth	-	-	Yes
Surface Night	Yes - using Radar	Yes - using Radar	-

ENCLOSURE (A)

CONFIDENTIAL Ww

Subject: U.S.S. S-32 - Report of Sixth War Patrol.

7. SUMMARY OF ATTACKS: (Cont'd)

Attack	#1	#2	#3
Deep Submergence	Yes	-	-
Estimated draft target	10'	16'	14'
Torpedo depth setting	6'	4'	1 at 4'
Bow or stern shot	Bow	Bow	Bow
Track Angle	70° S.	90° P.	100° P.
Gyro Angle	0°	0°	0°
Estimate target speed	0-3	0	13 Knots
Firing interval	20 - 15 - 20 Sec.	10 Sec.	12 Sec.
Spread - amount, kind	Divergent 50% target lenght (See remarks in narrative)	Divergent 60% target length	Longitudinal 70% target length

8. ENEMY A/S MEASURES:

The only A/S measures encountered were after attack #1 on March 9, 1943. The second DD or CM passed over torpedo room as we passed 55 feet and then we received a close string of three depth charges. We went to 180 feet making 150 RPM necessary to maintain depth control. The A/S vessel made a constant speed of 240 RPM while listening. He would stop periodically for a period of from 2 - 3 seconds and then start up at same speed. At no time was echo-ranging used. The second depth charge attack was close, but astern. We evaded by slow course changes, constant speed at 180 to 200 feet depth. Enemy broke off hunt 12 minutes after attack, apparently going back to assist damaged ship. The listening ability of this A/S vessel was really too good for comfort, but after all sound conditions in this area is predominantly excellent. We never had any trouble hearing him. The light sighted on the night of March 15, 1943 may have been from an enemy submarine attempting to lure any of our own submarines in to his range for a night periscope attack. Weather conditions were ideal for such at this time.

9. MINE SWEEPING:

None encountered.

10. MAJOR DEFECTS EXPERIENCED:

(A) HULL.

(1) The sound well in torpedo room was found about 60 percent flooded on March 5, 1943. The water covered the train and

-22- ENCLOSURE (A)

CONFIDENTIAL

Ww

Subject: U.S.S. S-32 - Report of Sixth War Patrol.

- -

10. MAJOR DEFECTS EXPERIENCED (Cont'd)

hoist limit switches and the lower end casing of the train motor. The system was grounded electrically. The forward H.P. bottle well and sound well were pumped dry, and we found the packing gland around the sound head shaft had been completely unscrewed, the packing forced up and almost all the way out allowing sea water to pour in the room in a steady stream. The reason this leak was not heard by torpedo room personnel was due to the metal-canvas cover sound proofing the well. By the ingenuity and resourcefulness of the auxiliary gang the packing gland nut was forced down sufficiently to stem the flow of water to a trickle. After surfacing (subsequent decrease in sea pressure) the gland nut was finally placed in proper position and packing forced into place. It took constant effort for 13 hours to complete this work under cold and most disagreeable circumstances. The sound well is so restricted to free movement that any work done therein is under a great handicap. In this respect I wish to commend JUNKIN, J.C., MoMMlc, U.S.N. for his work. It was due to his continuous efforts that the job was satisfactorily completed.

It is inconceivable that such a packing gland fixture as a nut is used in this case. It appears collossally stupid that a screw gland nut is used around a shaft of this size that is constantly turning and thereby presenting every opportunity for it to be unscrewed and allow sea water to enter the pressure hull; especially since this nut was not locked in any manner. The only reason we did not have a torpedo room flooding too quickly for safety was the fact that the drive shaft from the hoisting gear passes so near the head shaft that it prevented the gland nut from riding up the shaft far enough to allow all the packing to be forced out. An entirely different gland should be installed, such as used on the periscope, so positive locking is obtained. At the present we have a jury rig lock (wire) to prevent the gland nut from backing out again.

(2) The depth charging on March 9, 1943 opened up a seam or loosened some rivets between #9 fuel oil tank and the main lub oil tank polluting our lub oil with fuel.

(B) RADIO AND SOUND

(1) The loop antenna gave no results at periscope depths and may be due to improper shielding. This will be thoroughly gone over during next refit period.

(2) The "JK-QC" head shaft was inoperative on March 18, 1943 and cause determined as unknown trouble in the gear box. We were unable to raise or lower the shaft by motor or hand. The motor turns freely.

- -

(C) RADAR

(1) On February 28 we experienced a wide trace and sometimes a double trace on screen. The following work was done: tightened many loose connections, fixed loose cap on fuse in control panel; this returned trace to screen. Found one condenser shorting out due to the plug protection cap of the Cathode ray tube pressing against condenser. Correcting this returned trace to normal shape. (Warning Note: The range indicator unit should be supported on 1/2" blocks when removed from case and worked on in an upright position because the Cathode ray tube socket protection cup extends beyond the bottom of cahssis about 1/16".) Changed several tubes in range indicator and the grass on screen was normal. The magnetron tube blower became very noisy but we decided to let it run for removal at sea was next to impossible. The noise probably caused by bad bearings.

On March 5 we got double trace on screen. This was caused by loose connections on the main terminal block of the receiver-transmitter unit. Noticed at this time that all leads were resting against the heater directly under leads. These leads were burned, serving loose and insulation burned through in several places. These leads were then reserved and suspended clear of heater. Several days later it was found necessary to remove this heater (CSF 63188 F) because the heat wasagain attacking lead insulation. On March 16 the pulse and pips tend to bounce too much. The Thyratron tube appears black and may have lost its efficiency. Hours in use 450 so replaced with spare. Equipment now functions properly.

The depth charge attack caused a large leak around packing of radar mast. A careful taking up on gland seemed to stop this leakage.

11. COMMUNICATIONS:

(A) NPG FOX SKED

We were unable to copy NPG while submerged at any time. This trouble we trace to poorly shielded loop antenna.

While on the surface, difficulty was experienced copying on all FOX SKEDS between 0600 - 0800 GCT. The low frequency during this time was too noisy. The 7000 band was entirely blocked by nearby Jap "Hashers". The 14000 band proved useless during these hours.

(B) SHIP - SHORE (4235 Kcs. SERIES)

Our first transmission occurred at 1525 GCT March 10th. This communication was made on 4235 Kcs through heavy Jap interference. NPR's signal overrode all interference to some exten

- -

11. COMMUNICATIONS (Cont'd)

and evidently ours did also. NPR and this vessel used a different cadence from the Japs and this helped greatly. It is amusing to note here that our operator told NPR strength 5 and the Jap's strength was 3 so NPR could go ahead. The Japs did not like this and at least two more Jap stations entered the contest and they were all plenty mad (we apparently got their goat). NPR answered our call-up within 3 minutes. All in all this communication was very satisfactory except for the fact that NPR did not receipt for the message properly thereby causing one extra transmission.

The second communication was at 1005 GCT, March 15th. NPR answered within four minutes, giving us a signal strength 3. After transmission NPR informed us strength 1. After sending a few Vs, NPR sent strength 4 and we again sent the message. Several repeats of portions were necessary before final receipt. This communication lagged on for 20 minutes. At 1040 GCT, NPR called and asked for a repeat of a portion of message. We resent the portion requested and got a receipt. Later we were called by NPR and asked to verify the encipherment of the text so we sent the message again. The encipherment was correct but we saw our message on the FOX SKED with external indicator "BUNEK" instead of "BINEK". This may be reason for request of verification. NPR's improper use of procedure and exceptionally poor operating indicated an incompetent operator on watch during the entire period of clearing our transmission of second message.

The third communication was at 1159 GCT, March 16th. The first callup was to NPR on 4235 Kcs. No answer. The next callup was to NPC - no answer. Next callup was to NPG - no answer. We shifted receiver to 8470 Kcs and called again on 4235 Kcs and we heard NPM answer. We finally delivered message to NPM. Japanese interference on this particular night made copying on 4235 Kcs absolutely impossible at this end.

Last consecutive serial sent - VIEW COVE.
Last consecutive serial receiver - ULITKA CAPE.

12. SOUND CONDITIONS AND DENSITY LAYERS

Sound conditions were excellent. We experienced our old "YEHOODI" friend with pile driving noises interspersed. A recording of these noises was made on a magnetic wire recorder.

No density layers were noted.

CONFIDENTIAL Jk

Subject: U.S.S. S-32 - Report of Sixth War Patrol.

- -

13. HEALTH AND HABITABILITY:

Other than a few minor injuries and colds, which responded to routine treatment, requiring no admissions to the sick list, the health of the officers and crew was excellent. Vitamin pills were taken by all hands. It was noted that within a period of 24 hours following a depth charge attack, several cases of mild gastric disturbance consisting of slight nauseating and cramp-like feeling (actual nausea in only one case) developed; rapid recovery without treatment followed.

The winter clothing supplied still does not meet requirements for this area. Something should be done to provide proper clothing such as suggested by all commanding officers who have operated in this area. A fleece-lined coverall (waterproofed) would be excellent and less bulky than the conglomerate apparel now used. Aviation personnel seem to be well supplied with proper clothing so why can't we?

14. MILES STEAMED TO AND ENROUTE STATION:

(a) Dutch Harbor to area	700
(b) On station	1622
(c) Area to Dutch Harbor	700
Total	3022 miles.

15. FUEL OIL EXPENDED

(a) Dutch Harbor to area	3810
(b) On station	8977
(c) Area to Dutch Harbor	4030
Total	16,817 gallons.

16. FACTORS OF ENDURANCE REMAINING:

Torpedoes	Fuel	Provisions	Fresh Water	Personnel
3	11,383	7	Self-sustaining	6

17. FACTOR CAUSING END OF THIS PATROL:

Orders of Operation Order.

18. REMARKS:

The SJ Radar was invaluable to us on this patrol. It not only assisted materially in our attacks but enabled us to

- 26 - ENCLOSURE (A)

CONFIDENTIAL

Jk

Subject: U.S.S. S-32 - Report of Sixth War Patrol.

18. REMARKS (Cont'd)

navigate during darkness with full confidence near the bays and harbors of ATTU. The fathometer was another welcome addition to this vessel and without it our submerged reconnaissances could not have been made so near land without fear of hitting the beach. The keel-mounted JK-QC head with full control in the control room was most welcome to the Commanding Officer especially for evasive tactics during our depth charging on March 9th.

The entire crew seemed in better spirits than ever before and no doubt due to our luck and a busy patrol.

The Commanding Officer desired to commend the officers and crew for their actions and devotion to duty that made all our attacks so successful.

ENCLOSURE (A)

TG16.5/A16-3 Jk

Serial 032 March 25, 1943.

CONFIDENTIAL

From: The Commander Task Group Sixteen point Five. (The Commander Submarine Squadron Forty-Five).
To : The Commander Submarine Force, Pacific Fleet.

Subject: U.S.S. S-32 - Report of Sixth War Patrol.

Enclosure: (A) Subject Report.

1. The Sixth War Patrol of the U.S.S. S-32 covered a period of twenty-four (24) days, of which sixteen (16) days were spent in the patrol area. The patrol was characterized by thorough coverage of the assigned area, alertness and aggressiveness. Three attack opportunities were presented against combatant ships and three successful attacks were made.

2. The following is an analysis of the attacks:

Attack No. 1.

This night surface attack on an enemy destroyer was aggressively conducted. It was pressed home to almost point blank range. Four torpedoes were fired and one hit obtained under the forward after turret. A time check indicates that the hit was obtained by the second torpedo fired which was fired with the largest lead. It is therefore believed that the other three torpedoes missed astern. The target was observed to be seriously afire two hours after the attack and shortly thereafter the fire disappeared, followed by three explosions heard on the bridge and in the boat. A close reconnaissance of Holtz Bay, Chichagof Harbor and Sarana Bay during the next four days and aircraft observations failed to disclose the presence of the target, indicating it had been destroyed.

The S-32 had a narrow escape from ramming by a second enemy destroyer, which approached undetected, and was saved by quick submergence after firing the fourth torpedo. This emphasizes the importance of a continual radar search during low visibility attacks and of lookouts guarding their assigned sectors regardless of the diversion.

Attack No. 2.

This night surface attack on an enemy submarine was made on the assumption that the target was lying to, which assumption proved correct. Two torpedoes were fired and one hit obtained. It is believed the first torpedo missed ahead. At a range of 2500 yards, three or even four torpedoes would have been justified, considering the importance of the target. A thorough search of the area after firing by sound, radar, and visual and one positive hit warrants a claim of sinking.

- 1 - ENCLOSURE (B)

TG16.5/A16-3 Jk

Serial 032

CONFIDENTIAL

Subject: U.S.S. S-32 - Report of Sixth War Patrol.

- -

Attack No. 3.

This was a submerged daylight attack on an enemy submarine. Three torpedoes were fired and one hit obtained. The estimated range by periscope was 2500 yards. Range by time of explosion was 3000 yards. This long range hit on a 13 knot target demonstrates the value of a straight bow shot. The fact that an internal fire, followed by an observed disappearance and simultaneous sound report of stoppage of propellers, indicates the destruction of this submarine.

3. The S-32 is credited with destruction of one enemy destroyer or mine layer and two enemy submarines. This is based on the Action Report analysis of the attacks and evidence adduced by conversation with the Commanding Officer and the other officers attached to the vessel.

4. The material condition, upon return from patrol, was excellent. A thorough inspection of the hull and fittings will be conducted to determine if any undisclosed damage was inflicted by the depth charge attack. The evident unsatisfactory installation of the packing gland nut around the sound head shaft will be made the subject of a special report.

5. The radar was invaluable on this patrol and was intelligently used. In this connection, it is worthy of note that the alterations being made in the Sugar-class submarine, namely, SJ Radar, fathometer, JK-QC Sound Gear, Kleinschmidt evaporator, and the spider type conning tower hatch, have greatly enhanced the military value of these vessels.

6. The Commanding Officer, officers and crew of the S-32 are congratulated upon a well conducted patrol and for the following damage inflicted upon the enemy:

SUNK

1 Destroyer or Mine Layer	1200 tons
1 Submarine (I-121 or I-52 class)	1142 or 1390 tons
1 Submarine (I-1 class)	1955 tons

Recommendations for awards will be made to The Commander North Pacific Force.

ENCLOSURE (B)

2nd copy

FF12-10/A16-3(5)/(16) SUBMARINE FORCE, PACIFIC FLEET 1d

Serial 0645

DECLASSIFIED

Care of Fleet Post Office,
San Francisco, California,
May 18, 1943.

COMSUBPAC PATROL REPORT NO. 180
U.S.S. S-32 - SEVENTH WAR PATROL.

Reg. No. 13667
S.S. No. 6 0155

From: The Commander Submarine Force, Pacific Fleet.
To : Submarine Force, Pacific Fleet.

Subject: U.S.S. S-32 (SS137) - Report of Seventh War Patrol.

Enclosure: (A) Copy of Subject War Patrol Report.
(B) Copy of ComTaskGroup 16.5 (CSS 45) Conf. ltr. TG16.5/A16-3, serial 046 of April 26, 1943.

1. The Seventh War Patrol of the U.S.S. S-32 was the second successive successful one. Again, in spite of extremely severe Arctic weather, the S-32 carried out an aggressive, thorough, and efficient patrol. The remarks made by the Commander Task Group Sixteen point Five in his endorsement are concurred in by the Commander Submarine Force, Pacific Fleet.

2. The Commanding Officer, officers, and crew of the S-32 are congratulated for their aggressive and successful war patrol.

3. The Commander Task Force Sixteen is requested to credit the S-32 with the damage inflicted upon the enemy as stated in paragraph 6 of enclosure (B).

J. H. BROWN, Jr.,
Acting.

DISTRIBUTION:
(1M-43)
List III, SS.
Special:
P1(5), EN3(5), Z1(5),
Comsublant (2), X3(1),
Comsubsowespac (2),
Subschool, NL (2),
Comtaskfor 72 (2),
Comsubron 50 (2),
Comsopac (2),
Cinclant (2),
Comtaskfor 16 (1).

COMMANDER IN CHIEF U.S. FLEET

E. R. Swinburne
E. R. SWINBURNE,
Flag Secretary.

49788 FILMED

CONFIDENTIAL Jk

U.S.S. S-32 -- Report of Seventh War Patrol.

Period From -- March 29, 1943 to April 20, 1943.

OPERATION ORDER: Commander Task Group Sixteen Point Five Operation Order 11-43.

PROLOGUE:

Commenced refit period at SUBMARINE BASE, DUTCH HARBOR on March 20, 1943. Strategical situation caused a high-gear refit period and only the most essential work items were completed in order to commence next patrol on March 29, 1943. The SUBMARINE BASE worked shifts and in conjunction with ship's force all main work items were completed and ship fully ready for sea on March 29, 1943. Ship not depermed or wiped. No training period.

1. NARRATIVE:

29 March 1943 1315 (W)	Underway from DUTCH HARBOR in accordance with Comtaskgroup 16.5 Operation Order 11-43 and Operation Plan 3-42. Surface escort, "PHOEBE" YP57, proceeding out of harbor via swept channel.
1457 (W)	Arrived point XRAY and changed course to 270° true.
1504 (W)	Submerged for trim and deep dive for tightness check. Satisfactory.
1524 (W)	Surfaced. Dismissed surface escort and took departure for patrol area.
1613 (W)	Sighted twin engine Army transport plane bearing 180° true, on course East. Recognition signals were exchanged.
1932 (W)	Sighted BOGOSLOF ISLAND and at
2132 (W)	Passed BOGOSLOF ISLAND abeam to port distance 4 miles. Seas are very rough and we are unable to maintain speeds over 2/3 into seas. The icing conditions are terrible. The entire topside is covered with heavy ice.
30 March 1943 0632 (W)	Submerged for twilight and also to de-ice the ship.
1945 (W)	Submerged for twilight and also to de-ice the ship. Seas were very high all day and our progress slow.

CONFIDENTIAL Jk.

Subject: U.S.S. S-32 - Report of Seventh War Patrol.

---

31 March 1943

0935 (W) Seas are moderating so went ahead standard speed. Air temperature rose 10° F., and icing conditions are past. Will not make twilight dives for it is considered most essential to reach area as soon as possible in order to not leave it uncovered any longer than necessary. The S-23 is due to depart our area at dark tonight.

1 April 1943

1615 (W) Sighted PBY plane bearing 340° true on course 100° true, distance 8 miles. apparently plane crew failed to spot us for he soon disappeared into poor area of visibility.

1700 (W) Entered patrol area and commenced surface patrol towards HOLTZ BAY.

2 April 1943

0648 (W) Sighted ATTU ISLAND bearing 180° true distance 11 miles.

0653 (W) Submerged for periscope patrol.

1100 (W) Changed zone time to plus eleven.

1330 (X) Heard one (1) distant explosion.

1345 (X) Suddenly all hell broke loose with a series of about 19 explosions and some sounded close. It brought all hands out of their bunks and battle stations were automatically manned before we were able to surmise that it might be a bombing mission to HOLTZ BAY causing this welcome. We were about 4 miles out from the bay and periscope observations showed puffs of smoke on the beach and clouds of dark smoke over the enemy camp area. No planes could be seen. All this certainly startled us and I wish we had prior information of such attacks in our area for the following reasons:

(a) We could observe for damage.
(b) We could be in best position to intercept any fleeing ships (if any).
(c) We would not be so startled and lose time wondering what it was all about.
(d) Considered good judgment to let us know for coordination.

- 2 - ENCLOSURE (A)

CONFIDENTIAL Jk

Subject: U.S.S. S-32 - Report of Seventh War Patrol.

- -

2 April 1943 (Continued)

1347 (X) Heard two (2) more explosions.

1400 (X) Changed zone time to plus twelve.

1307 (Y) Took periscope photos of ATTU.

1615 (Y) Took periscope photos of ATTU.

2005 (Y) Surfaced. Commenced night surface patrol.

3 April 1943

0509 (Y) Submerged for periscope patrol. Seas are picking up. Best part of day spent well below periscope depth because of storm. Impossible to maintain periscope depth control satisfactorily.

2010 (Y) Surfaced in gale and forced to accept best course and speed to ride out gale while charging battery. In like cases it is not always possible to patrol on tracks considered best for coverage in area but "ole man weather" is hard to defy.

2300 (Y) Received message, presumably from task group commander, but unable to decode. Internal indicator must be wrong.

4 April 1943

0447 (Y) Received correction to message and it tells us about approaching enemy force. Believe we can be in excellent interception position all this day.

0513 (Y) Submerged for periscope patrol. Seas are still rough but not too bad.

1426 (Y) Took periscope photos of ATTU.

2015 (Y) Surfaced and commenced night surface patrol on a north-south track out from HOLTZ BAY.

2345 (Y) Received message from task group commander changing date in previous message. The enemy may have been able to slip in HOLTZ BAY during last night but I sincerely doubt it. Our radar went out of commission just after surfacing.

- 3 - ENCLOSURE (A)

Pn

CONFIDENTIAL

Subject: U.S.S. S-32 SEVENTH WAR PATROL

- -

5 April 1943

0300 (Y) Radar back in commission.

0503 (Y) Submerged about 6 miles north of HOLTZ BAY and will patrol across this entrance and CHICHAGOF HARBOR all day, as close in as possible.

1033 (Y) Took periscope photos of bays etc. The weather is excellent. Brilliant sun, seas moderate and visibility maximum.

1225 (Y) Heard 9 explosions and saw smoke rising from camp area in HOLTZ BAY.

1230 (Y) Heard about 23 explosions. None as loud as those on 2 April. There now appears to be a white smoke pall low to enemy camp area but no large fires observed.

1240 (Y) Took periscope photos of HOLTZ BAY.

2017 (Y) Surfaced. Wind about 30 knots but seas have not built up too much as yet to prevent fair results while patrolling on surface.

6 April 1943

0300 (Y) Seas picking up and a gale from the north is in view. Very cold and snow squalls intermittently.

0503 (Y) Submerged in full gale and headed towards HOLTZ BAY with intent of continuing on to STELLER COVE to investigate for submarine sighted in "ATTU COVE" by Army attacking planes of yesterday at 0730 (Y). There is no "ATTU COVE" so named on charts but we are assuming this may mean STELLER COVE. Investigation of this cove gave negative information. Periscope depth control is practically impossible without broaching.

2018 (Y) Surfaced in full gale and forced to accept best course and speed to ride it out while charging battery. Received message stating that submarine sighted by Army was in "ATTU ONE" instead of "ATTU COVE". There seems to be some lack of proper dissemination of information from aviation. We would certainly like to know the following (which

Pn

CONFIDENTIAL

Subject: U.S.S. S-32 SEVENTH WAR PATROL

- -

6 April 1943 (Continued)

2018 (Y) should have been available).

(a) Surface or submerged.
(b) Best position.
(c) Course and speed.
(d) Exact time.

NOTE: Who knows - it may have been us during one of our broaching moods.

7 April 1943

0456 (Y) Submerged in heavy gale and headed towards SARANA BAY. Depth control was night-marish all throughout the day. At one time we suddenly broached from 75 feet from a condition which seemed satisfactory at the time. We managed to go in and out of SARANA BAY but periscope observations poor.

2020 (Y) Surfaced - weather no change, and again forced to accept best course and speed on surface while charging battery. There certainly has been no let-up in weather for one long period.

8 April 1943

0500 (Y) Submerged - no change in weather and it appears to be another day of heavy rolling at any depth with accompanying prohibitive periscope exposures. We are all getting very sick and tired of this protracted bad weather spell. Even a good day between several bad ones is acceptable. Torpedo firing in this weather would be sheer folly. Heavy weather continued all day.

2030 (Y) Surfaced and forced to adhere to sea conditions for course and speed while charging battery.

2145 (Y) Starboard bridge lookout suffered possible rib fracture when huge wave carried him against hatch. Received treatment by pharmacist mate and turned in.

9 April 1943

0506 (Y) Submerged in moderate seas. We may get a break in the weather. Heavy snow squalls prevented close reconnaissance of harbors today.

- -

<u>9 April 1943</u>
1927 (Y) (Continued)
"Sound" got propeller contact bearing 240° true. According to D.R. this shows ship about 3 miles north of HOLTZ BAY, probably entering. Lost sound contact after 5 minutes. Heavy snow prevented periscope sighting.

2034 (Y) Surfaced. Seas behaving nicely tonight (comparatively speaking). Sent contact report to task force and group commander. Commenced patrol on surface north-south line out from HOLTZ BAY.

<u>10 April 1943</u>
0157 (Y) "Radar" bearing 135° true range 7000 yards (large image on screen 1/2 inch high). Went to battle stations and commenced approach. Weather: complete overcast, misty, dark and visibility poor. (Contact #1).

0207 (Y) "Radar" picked up second target (smaller image) to the left (ahead) of main target. Still unable to see targets at 3000 yards. Finally saw large ship at about 2600 yards and then smaller ship. The outline is very hazy and blurred but she is <u>very</u> large. Range decreasing to 2200 yards and ships apparently changed course from about 320° true to 270° true and we rapidly swung left to catch them before out of range. Target speed 14.5 knots.

0213-15 (Y) Fired first torpedo followed by others at following times: 02-13-25, 02-13-36, 02-13-38. Torpedoes 3 and 4 were fired only 2 seconds apart due to a control error in firing order. Number 3 was fired by electric and number 4 by hand.

0214 (Y) Changed course to the right to clear scene - radar tracking excellently and we started to open range.

02-15-09 (Y) Heard one very loud torpedo explosion. Heard and felt by bridge personnel and crew below and at ...

02-15-18 (Y) Heard the second torpedo explosion same as the first. Did not see anything from bridge - ships not in view. Continued evasive tactics on surface - radar still tracking nicely when at

02-18-50 Heard two (2) rumbling explosions (from bridge and below) characteristics not certain. Then at

Subject: U.S.S. S-32 - Report of Seventh War Patrol

- -

10 April 1943 (Continued)

0219 (Y) Radar operator reported all trace of ships suddenly vanished from the screen at range of 3,600 yards. This leads us to believe that the large ship must have sunk and the escort having streaked off on the surface at high speed. We changed course to head back and then settled on course 000° true. Constant radar and visual search remained negative.

0300 (Y) Secured from battle stations and continued one engine speed patrol and one engine battery charge. Sent contact report to task force and group commander.

0458 (Y) Submerged and proceeded towards HOLTZ BAY.

1050 (Y) Sighted PBY plane bearing 000° true on course east distance about 6,000 yards. Took periscope photos during day between snow squalls.

1200 (Y) Took periscope photos of HOLTZ BAY and ATTU northern coast line. No enemy activity seen in the bay.

2035 (Y) Surfaced in a moderate sea and clear moonlight night.

11 April 1943

0458 (Y) Submerged and patrolled along northern coast of ATTU and across HOLTZ BAY and CHICHAGOF HARBOR. Visibility never very good throughout the day.

2038 (Y) Surfaced in a moderate sea. Snow squalls and periods of excellent visibility throughout the night.

12 April 1943

0457 (Y) Submerged and patrolled along northern coast of ATTU and bays. Visibility varied throughout the day from fair to poor. Watered batteries today. Made close reconnaissance of SARANA BAY, CHICHAGOF HARBOR and HOLTZ BAY. Took periscope photos. Negative information on enemy.

2030 (Y) Surfaced. Clear moonlight night with occasional snow squalls.

13 April 1943

0452 (Y) Submerged and patrolled same as yesterday. Visibility excellent throughout day.

CONFIDENTIAL

1d

Subject: U.S.S. S-32 - Report of Seventh War Patrol.

- -

13 April 1943 (Continued)

2040 (Y) Surfaced in another clear moonlight night. In fact it seemed nearly as light as day. Visibility excellent.

14 April 1943

0454 (Y) Submerged. Proceeded towards western part of ATTU in order to get periscope photos of this section. Have been unable to get good results before due to poor visibility. We were able to get some good low power periscope photos in the afternoon.

2045 (Y) Surfaced in the calmest seas ever found by us in this area. Bright moonlight and excellent visibility. Patrolled on a north-south line from STELLER COVE.

15 April 1943

0445 (Y) Submerged and headed towards HOLTZ BAY. Visibility poor due to rain and snow squalls. Seas calm. We are missing task group commander's WILLIAM series. We have received three despatches since this series. The last despatch ordered us to return to base in accordance with current operation order. Patrolled on an east-west line just north of the entrance to HOLTZ BAY and CHICHAGOF HARBOR. Took periscope photos.

2047 (Y) Surfaced. Bright, clear moonlight night. Seas moderate and visibility excellent, except for occasional snow squalls. Spent the night patrolling north and south.

16 April 1943

0455 (Y) Submerged and headed towards HOLTZ BAY.

1048 (Y) While about 2 miles from the bay heard, and felt, a series of 15 explosions. Some seemed distant and others nearer. They sounded like depth charges but the time interval between the "ping" and the explosion was too short. Believe this was a bombing mission to ATTU. At this time we were enveloped in a snow squall and could see nothing. About 10 minutes later the snow cleared but we could see no evidence of bombing in the bays or anywhere along the coast. There was an interval of about 5 seconds between explosions - not a rapid fire type that we heard on April 2.

1048 (Y) Patrolled across the entrance to HOLTZ BAY and CHICHAGOF HARBOR and then headed north and then east. Evidence of enemy activity negative.

Subject: U.S.S. S-32 - Report of Seventh War Patrol.

- -

16 April 1943 (Continued)

2043 (Y) Surfaced - commenced night patrol and set course for track assigned to DUTCH HARBOR.

17 April 1943

0200 (Y) Changed zone time to plus eleven.

0539 (Y) Submerged for twilight.

0600 (X) Left patrol area.

0635 (X) Surfaced. Commenced zig-zag plan on surface at standard speed.

0801 (X) Sighted PBY on course 270° true, bearing 020° true distance 6 miles. No exchange of signals and apparently plane did not sight us.

1253 (X) Sighted PBY on course 270° true bearing 245° true distance 8 miles. No exchange of signals and apparently plane did not sight us.

1443 (X) Sighted PBY on course 090° true bearing 225° true distance 5 miles. No exchange of signals and apparently plane did not sight us.

2200 (X) Changed zone time to plus ten.

18 April 1943

0350 (W) Sighted 2 ships bearing 070° true distance about 12,000 yards. Visibility excellent at the time. Radar could not pick them up. From known information these should be the light cruisers of our own surface forces. Position and course checks satisfactorily. Lost ships in a snow squall about 20 minutes later.

0555 (W) Submerged for twilight.

0630 (W) Surfaced.

19 April 1943

0543 (W) Submerged for twilight.

0620 (W) Surfaced. Continued base course and speed - zig-zagging.

CONFIDENTIAL

Rs

Subject: U.S.S. S-32 Report of Seventh War Patrol.

- -

19 April 1943 (Continued)

0853 (W) Sighted PBY plane bearing 152° true distance 9 miles on course 090° true. Plane apparently failed to sight us.

0846 (W) Sighted land bearing 164° true.

1046 (W) Sighted PBY plane bearing 207° true distance 7 miles on course 270° true. Plane apparently failed to sight us.

1552 (W) Sighted 3 ships hull down bearing 040° true distance 10 miles. These ships later proved to be friendly (AP, PG and ODD) which we expected to intercept in accordance with information previously received from task group commander. Recognition signals were exchanged.

1753 (W) Sighted BOGOSLOF ISLAND bearing 070° true distance 22 miles. Visibility has been maximum all day and seas very moderate with slight swells.

2032 (W) Passed BOGOSLOF abeam to port 2 1/2 miles.

2052 (W) Sighted 4 friendly ships hull down bearing 170° true. We had been previously notified of their presence by task group commander.

2236 (W) Sighted searchlight, on beach, bearing 165° true.

2245 (W) Sighted steady white light on beach, bearing 190° true.

20 April 1943

0610 (W) Exchanged recognition signals with surface escort (YP57).

0930 (W) Arrived SUBMARINE BASE, DUTCH HARBOR.

CONFIDENTIAL Rs

Subject: U.S.S. S-32 Report of Seventh War Patrol.

2. WEATHER:

March 29 - April 2, 1943. Enroute DUTCH HARBOR to ATTU ISLAND.

Weather was generally quite cold, below freezing most of the time, causing ice to form on superstructure. Sky was generally overcast at night permitting few morning and evening twilight fixes. Sun during day however broke through enough to obtain running fixes every day. During passage seas were fairly calm compared to usual rough weather in the area. A weak southerly set was encountered making it necessary to steer about two (2) degrees to the north of our course.

April 2 - 16, 1943. On station in vicinity of ATTU.

The period from April 2, to April 10, was almost continually rough and snow fell incessantly. About four days out of this period the seas were mountainous, making periscope exposures impossible and depth control very hard. Continous snow storms passed through area making visibility very bad about seventy-five percent of the time. These snow storms could be seen coming in from the north. The latter few days on station proved quite a change. The snow storms became more infrequent, part of them being in the form of rain. The heavy swells and mountainous seas became long low swells, and at times almost calm. The moon made visibility very good at night the last few days as the island could be observed from distances as great as 15 to 20 miles. The wind and seas were generally from north-west to north-east changing rapidly at times. Wind, except for a few of the roughest days, was moderate, also coming from a north west to northeasterly direction.

April 16 - 20, 1943. Enroute ATTU ISLAND to DUTCH HARBOR.

Weather very mild, seas calm and visibility excellent during both day and night except for a few scattered snow storms which last only a few minutes at a time. Star fixes were obtained, also running fixes of the sun during day.

3. TIDAL INFORMATION:

In the ATTU area the southeasterly currents are still encountered. The set and drift recordings were always between 100° true and 150° true and from 0.7 to 1.0 knots. The current around the center of the island is more east by south east while along the east and west extremities of ATTU the current is more southeast. A definate southerly current is still obtained off entrance of HOLTZ BAY. Also a very strong current is experienced off CAPE WRANGELL. In order to make good a course at 200° true, we had to steer about 20° to the right (220° true).

 ENCLOSURE (A)

CONFIDENTIAL Rs

Subject: U.S.S. S-32 Report of Seventh War Patrol.

- -

4. NAVIGATIONAL AIDS:

Charts made available this vessel, though of great use with aerial photos, topography and a few soundings, are still inadequate for navigation close to the shore.

During this patrol, the north coast of ATTU was covered and a series of periscope pictures were taken from known positions. SARANA BAY, CHICHAGOF HARBOR, and HOLTZ BAY were covered thoroughly by periscope pictures.

Also, soundings were taken along the north coast of the island and plotted on a chart.

By means of study of various available charts, periscope observations, and fixes, we believe the major discrepancy of charts of this area has been found. The entire north coast of the island from HOLTZ BAY to CAPE WRANGELL should be moved northward about two miles. A chart showing what we believe the correct coast line of Northern ATTU has been constructed. Separate charts showing soundings taken, photos taken, and corrected coast of ATTU has been delivered to Comtaskgroup 16.5.

5. DESCRIPTION OF ENEMY SHIPS:

Contact	Date Time	Position	Course	Speed	Description
1.	4-10-43 0157 Y.	Lat. 53°-12'-30"N. Long. 173°-05'-00" E.	330° true	14.5 K.	Visibility was so poor - misty and hazy - that a clear outline was prevented. From the general blurry outline of the two (2) ships it was believed that the very large one was a supply ship of about 9000 tons and the smaller ship was a DD or patrol type escort vessel. No masts or bridge superstructure could be made out; the entire shape was just a rectangular blurred shape.

- 12 - ENCLOSURE (A)

- -

6. AIRCRAFT SIGHTED:

Contact	Date Time	Type	Position	Course	Altitude	Remarks
1.	3-29-43 1613W.	2 Eng: Army Trans-port.	Lat.54°-05' N. Long.166°-41' W.	090°	3000'	Recognition signals exchanged.
2.	4-1-43 1615W.	PBY	Lat.54°-03' N. Long.174°-58' E.	100°	1000'	Plane apparently did not sight us. Distance 8 miles.
3.	4-10-43 1050X.	PBY	Lat.53°-01' N. Long.173°-15' E.	090°	1000'	Sighted plane while we were submerged.
4.	4-17-43 0801X	PBY	Lat.53°-20' N. Long.175°-33' E.	270°	2000'	Plane apparently did not sight us. Distance 6 miles.
5.	4-17-43 1253X	PBY	Lat.53°-26' N. Long.176°-49' E.	270°	2000'	Plane apparently did not sight us. Distance 8 miles.
6.	4-17-43 1443 X	PBY	Lat.53°-27' N. Long.177°-18' E.	090°	2000'	Plane apparently did not sight us. Distance 5 miles.
7.	4-19-43 0853W	PBY	Lat. 53°-42' N. Long.177°-52' E.	090°	2000'	Plane apparently did not sight us. Distance 9 miles.
8.	4-19-43 1046W.	PBY	Lat.54°-43' N. Long.177°-25' E.	270°	3000'	Plane apparently did not sight us. Distance 7 miles.

ENCLOSURE (A)

CONFIDENTIAL

Subject: U.S.S. S-32 - Report of Seventh War Patrol

7. SUMMARY OF ATTACKS:

Attack	#1
Date	4-10-43
Location - latitude	53°-12'-30" N.
longitude	173°-05'-00" E.
Torpedoes fired on each attack	4
Hits	2
Number sunk (tonnage)	-
Number damaged or probably sunk	9000 (?)
Type of target	Supply ship (?)
Range 1500 yards or less	-
Range more than 1500 yards	1950
Periscope depth	-
Surface night	Yes
Deep submergence	-
Estimated draft target	26'
Torpedo depth setting	4'
Bow or stern shot	Bow
Track angle	90 Port
Gyro angle	0°
Estimate target speed	14.5 Knots
Firing interval	10-9-2 seconds (see remarks).
Spread - amount kind	Longitudinal 50% target length.
Remarks	(See narrative).

8. ENEMY A/S MEASURES:

None encountered. The two ships sighted and attacked the early morning of 10 April, 1943 were not zig-zagging and making a speed of 14.5 knots. The escort vessel was ahead of escorted ship but not more than 500 yards. There was no evidence of echoranging. After the attack we remained on the surface and there was no evidence of counter attacks, unless the two explosions after torpedo explosions were depth charges. Individual opinions on board this ship vary as to what type explosions were heard after the torpedo explosions.

9. MINE SWEEPING:

None encountered.

10. MAJOR DEFECTS EXPERIENCED:

A. ENGINEERING.
At 0445 (Y) on 12 April the water jacket gage for the starboard C&R air compressor registered excessive pressure and jammed. The compressor was immediately secured. The first stage cooler coils were removed and tested under 100 pounds pressure. A split, about four inches long, was discovered

ENCLOSURE (A)

- -

10. MAJOR DEFECTS EXPERIENCED: Engineering. (Continued)

on the inner side of the first coil 90° from the compressor first stage discharge nipple. A soft patch was installed, made up by four layers of plain linen tape impregnated with copaltite, and then served with sail twine smeared with copaltite. The coil was tested satisfactorily. At 2100 the compressor was tested and a leak showed again. The cooler coil was removed and another split was found at the opposite end of the coil of same size and in same position except it was 90° from second stage suction nipple. A similar soft patch was applied. The cooler was tested satisfactorily and replaced. The compressor was run for 45 minutes and all repairs appeared to be satisfactory. Placed compressor in commission.

B. Sound Equipment.

Poor installation of the train limit switch for the keel mounted "JK-QC" head has caused trouble on numerous occassions. The limit switch allows the head to be trained too far. This excessive train allowance usually winds the cable leads to become fouled under the train gear. Of course the most logical and best solution is to arrange the leads in a proper manner to prevent this instead of curtailing the train arc but lack of space in the well places this correction beyond the capacity of our ship's force. During the last refit period the leads were renewed with improper type of cables, The correct type of cable was not available at DUTCH HARBOR and some was ordered from KODIAK. Replacement ordered failed to arrive during short refit period. The cables used for replacement were smaller and inferior in insulation and armor and are much more susceptable to catching in the gears. In spite of careful tending this trouble appeared again during this patrol and a splice job was necessitated.

During an inspection for a ground it was noticed that transformer (T-104) located in WCA-1 driver unit was leaking oil. The transformer casing was cleaned and blow holes in the casting were sealed with copaltite. Very little oil had leaked out and the equipment functioned properly during the remainder of the patrol.

This ship was not issued any spare parts for the newly installed sound equipment. To date no spare parts have been received and it means replacement with improper or inferior equipment as necessary, if even such can be obtained.

C. Radar.

On April 4, the radar suddenly quit and all meters read zero except the regulated voltage meter which read 400 volts instead

Go

CONFIDENTIAL

REPORT OF U.S.S. S-32 SEVENTH WAR PATROL

- -

10. MAJOR DEFECTS EXPERIENCED: Radar (Continued)

of the normal 280 volts. This indicated that the 110 volt A.C. was not being taken from that source and the fuses in the system supplying the filament circuit were blown. A complete check was made and investigation revealed the fuses in the 110 volt A.C. circuit supplying the antenna system were not blown. These fuses are of the same rating as those found blown and the entire antenna circuit seemed isolated from the 110 volt filament circuit. The cause for these blown fuses could not be determined. It is very urgent that a suitable sweat guard be installed to protect the antenna contacts. We have to dry and clean these contacts and plates daily prior surfacing.

On 17 April we found the bearing indicator reading about 30 degrees off from the true bearing of antenna mirror. We managed to correct this error to within one degree but the cause for the error is undetermined. Something may have slipped inside the bearing indicator housing.

11. COMMUNICATIONS:

A. NPG FOX SKED.
The signal strength on low frequency was good but the noise level too high; believed due to ship installation.

The high frequency was used very nearly throughout patrol and reception very good.

B. NPM FOX SKED.
This schedule was guarded for the first 15 minutes after each odd hour while submerged. No messages were received. At times reception was possible but ordinarily the noise level was too high for perfect reception.

C. SHIP-SHORE.
All our transmissions from patrol area were taken by NPM and the results were excellent, the best one could hope for. The transmissions went off in the absolute minimum time and the operators at NPM certainly knew their business. Our operators states it is a joy to work under such conditions and cooperation. NPM is certainly on its toes. All transmissions were effected on 4235 KCS.

The usual constant JAPANESE "hashing" was encountered but certainly did not hamper our communications.

LAST SERIAL RECEIVED - LEMON POINT
LAST SERIAL SENT - ZIP ROCK.

- 16 - ENCLOSURE (A)

CONFIDNETIAL

REPORT OF U.S.S. S-32 SEVENTH WAR PATROL

- -

12. SOUND CONDITIONS AND DENSITY LAYERS:

Sound conditions were excellent, as usual in this area. No density layers noted.

13. HEALTH AND HABITABILITY:

A marked lowered resistance of the personnel resulting in an increase of common colds and coughs was apparent. The fact that only one week was spent in port for a refit period between the last patrol and the present one plus an increasing time submerged may account for this condition.

One night lookout was injured during a heavy gale; examination revealed contusion of the left lower chest wall, (rib fracture suspected) - adhesive strapping applied and man put to bed. This treatment apparently effective and no further complaints from patient. He was back to duty 24 hours later.

In general the health of the personnel may be considered good and there was no illness or injuries of a serious nature.

We are still sadly lacking the proper clothing for patrols in this area.

14. MILES STEAMED TO AND ENROUTE STATION:

(a) Dutch Harbor to area	834
(b) On station	1616
(c) Area to Dutch Harbor	817
Total	3267 miles.

15. FUEL OIL EXPENDED:

(a) Dutch Harbor to area	3750
(b) On station	7550
(c) Area to Dutch Harbor	4690
Total	15,990 gallons.

16. FACTORS OF ENDURANCE REMAINING:

Torpedoes	Fuel	Provisions	Fresh Water	Personnel
8	12,710	7	Self-sustaining	7

17. FACTOR CAUSING END OF THIS PATROL:

Orders of Operation Order.

- 17 - ENCLOSURE (A)

- -

18. REMARKS

The "SJ" radar was again most valuable on this patrol. It is apparent that the JAPANESE play the weather and visibility conditions to get supply ships to ATTU. For this reason it should be assumed that **practically** all contacts will materialize at night or during periods of very low visibility during the daylight period. The season for fog is about here so surface - radar patrols (daylight) may reap rewards. I am convinced that we would have missed our one and only contact if our radar had not detected them.

It should be of interest to note that of the six (6) patrol planes sighted by us while on the surface none gave evidence of seeing us - and we did not submerge to escape detection.

The Commanding Officer desires to commend the officers and crew for their continued devotion to duty and can state that their actions have been in accordance with the highest traditions of the Naval Service.

TG16.5/A16-3

Rs

Serial 046

April 26, 1943.

CONFIDENTIAL

From: The Commander Task Group Sixteen point Five. (The Commander Submarine Squadron Forty-Five.)
To : The Commander Submarine Force, Pacific Fleet.

Subject: U.S.S. S-32 - Report of Seventh War Patrol.

Enclosure: (A) Subject Report.

1. The Seventh War Patrol of the U.S.S. S-32 covered a period of twenty-three (23) days, of which fifteen (15) days were spent in the patrol area. The patrol, as usual with this submarine, was characterized by thorough coverage of the assigned area, alertness and aggressiveness. A successful attack was made on the only contact presented.

2. The following is an analysis of the attack:

This night surface attack was made during extremely low visibility. The target was picked up at 7000 yards by radar and was not sighted until the radar range recorded 1950 yards, at which range four torpedoes were fired and two hits obtained. A time check indicates that the first and second torpedoes hit. It is believed that the third and the fourth torpedoes missed astern due to an under estimation of the speed. Although the target was not actually seen to sink, because of low visibility, it was tracked by radar to 3600 yards, at which range the image disappeared suddenly from the screen, indicating its destruction.

3. The S-32 is credited with sinking one unidentified enemy cargo ship of an estimated 9000 tons. This is based on the Action Report analysis of the attack and evidence adduced from conversation with the Commanding Officer and the other officers attached to the vessel.

4. It is interesting to note that six (6) patrol planes were sighted by the S-32 while on the surface at estimated ranges of five (5) to nine (9) miles and altitudes 1000 to 3000 feet without any indication that the submarine was sighted by the planes.

5. The periscope pictures and other navigational data obtained on this patrol were forwarded to the Commander North Pacific Force for his information. The reconnaissance was very thorough and furnished valuable information of enemy occupied territory.

ENCLOSURE (B)

TG16.5/A16-3

Rs

Serial 046

April 26, 1943

CONFIDENTIAL

Subject: U.S.S. S-32 - Report of Seventh War Patrol.

- -

6. The Commanding Officer, officers and crew of the S-32 are congratulated upon an alert and aggressive patrol and for the following damage inflicted upon the enemy:

SUNK

1 Unidentified Cargo Vessel 9000 tons (estimated)

- 2 - ENCLOSURE (B)

1st copy

Reg. No. 15279
S.S. No. 0767
1d

FF12-10/A16-3(5)/(16) SUBMARINE FORCE, PACIFIC FLEET

Serial 0761

CONFIDENTIAL DECLASSIFIED

Care of Fleet Post Office,
San Francisco, California,
June 19, 1943.

COMSUBSPAC PATROL REPORT NO. 197
U.S.S. S-32 - EIGHTH WAR PATROL.

From: The Commander Submarine Force, Pacific Fleet.
To : Submarine Force, Pacific Fleet.

Subject: U.S.S. S-32 (SS137) - Report of Eighth War Patrol.

Enclosure: (A) Copy of Comtaskgroup 16.5 (CSS 45) Conf. ltr. TG16.5/A16-3, Serial 057 of June 8, 1943.
(B) Copy of Subject War Patrol Report.

1. The Commander Submarine Force, Pacific Fleet, concurs in the remarks as expressed by the Commander Task Group Sixteen point Five in enclosure (A).

C. A. LOCKWOOD, Jr.

DISTRIBUTION:
(Complete Reports)

Cominch	(5)
VCNO	(5)
Cincpac	(5)
Cinclant	(2)
Comsubslant	(8)
S/M School, NL	(2)
Comsopac	(2)
Comsowespac	(1)
Comsubssowespac	(2)
CTF 72	(2)
CTF 16	(1)
Comsubspac	(10)
SUBAD, M.I.	(2)
Comsubcomsubpac Midway	(2)
All Squadron and Div. Commanders, Subspac	(2)
U.S.S. S-32	(1)

(COMSUBSPAC Endorsement only:)
All Submarines, Subspac (1)

R. C. LAWVER,
Flag Secretary.

51536 FILMED

TG16.5/A16-3

Serial 057

June 8, 1943

CONFIDENTIAL

From: The Commander Task Group Sixteen point Five. (The Commander Submarine Squadron Forty-Five).

To : The Commander Submarine Force, Pacific Fleet.

Subject: U.S.S. S-32 - Eighth War Patrol.

1. The Eighth War Patrol of the S-32 covered a period of twenty days, of which five days were spent in the patrol area. The entire time on station was marked with poor visibility, which is a tremendous handicap when operating in waters frequented by neutral vessels.

2. The decision of the Commanding Officer in breaking off the attack on a vessel identified as Russian, May 15, is concurred in. It is reported that neutral vessels are not carrying adequate identification. This cannot help but hamper the Commanding Officer in retaining his initial advantage.

3. The patrol was terminated because of casualty to the port main motor. The S-32 is scheduled for navy yard overhaul commencing August 1. The performance of SJ radar has been generally satisfactory in this Squadron. Full allowance of radar spares has been received recently at Submarine Base, Dutch Harbor.

4. The morale of the crew upon return from patrol was noticeably high. It is unfortunate that poor visibility and curtailed time on station greatly hindered the fruitfulness of this patrol.

ENCLOSURE (A)

CONFIDENTIAL

1d

U.S.S. S-32 - Report of Eighth War Patrol. Period from May 4, 1943 to May 23, 1943. Operation Order, Commander Task Group Sixteen point Five Operation Order No. 18-43.

PROLOGUE

Arrived at SUBMARINE BASE, DUTCH HARBOR from seventh war patrol on Tuesday, April 20, 1943. Commenced refit on April 21, using base repair force and relief crew from Submarine Squadron Forty-Five.

On May 2, 1943, Lieutenant Commander M. G. SCHMIDT, U.S.N., was relieved by Lieutenant F. J. HARLFINGER, U.S.N., as commanding officer. Completed refit. Ready for sea May 4, 1943.

1. NARRATIVE

May 4, 1943

0855(W) Departed DUTCH HARBOR with escort AM 184.

1030(W) Released escort at point XRAY as he was useless in mountainous seas and low visibility. He had been unable to keep up with us for the past hour.

1217(W) Went ahead standard speed on both engines going through AKUTAN PASS, to reduce the flow of water down the conning tower hatch from the following seas.

1300(W) Commenced surface patrol on north and south line south of AKUTAN PASS as directed by Commander Task Group Sixteen point Five.

May 5, 1943

0300(X) Took departure for patrol area.

May 6, 1943 to May 12, 1943 Enroute patrol area on the surface patrolling across possible JAPANESE reinforcement routes to KISKA and ATTU. Passage was extremely rough and stormy with almost zero visibility the greater percentage of the time. One star fix and three running fixes of sun were obtained during entire passage to area. Training dives, fire control drills, and gunnery practices were held daily when weather permitted. New air cooled .50 cal. machine guns were tried and adjusted. These two guns would be a tremendous advantage in a battle surface, and it is suggested that they be made standard equipment for S-boats.

May 12, 1943

1400(Y) Entered patrol area having had no navigational "fixes" since 7 May.

May 13, 1943

0516(Y) Submerged to attempt repair of SJ Radar which was out of commission. (Very rough seas prevented work on surface).

ENCLOSURE (B)

CONFIDENTIAL

Hn

Subject: U.S.S. S-32 - Report of Eight War Patrol.

- -

13 May 1943 (Continued)

1312 (Y) Surfaced, visibility reduced to about two miles, heavy seas, radar still out of commission.

1457 (Y) Sighted land bearing 300°T, crossed line of bearing with sun line and determined position as ten miles south east of ONEKOTAN TO ISLAND. We had been set about forty miles to the south. Set course for ONEKOTAN KAIKYO. Submerged to repair radar as seas were too rough to attempt repair on surface.

2105 (Y) Surfaced, radar still out of commission, visibility poor due to rain and snow.

14 May 1943

0830 (Y) Having reached an estimated point 12 miles southeast of KARABU ZAKI PARAMISHIRU (in a pea soup fog) changed course to 270°T. to start a surface patrol across MUSASHI WAN and the strait of ONEKOTAN KAIKYO.

1028 (Y) Fog lifted - sighted land bearing 096, 232, 256, 310° gyro which made it all seem in a erroneous position. Immediately took a rough azimuth and found a 54° westerly error in gyro. Magnetic compass at this time is acting very erratic. Position obtained from corrected bearings showed us to be about seven miles north of ONEKOTAN TO ISLAND and on western edge of ONEKOTAN KAIKYO. By back tracking position, found that we had passed about four miles south of MUSASHI WAN while going through strait. Steered by wind and sea while repairs were effected to gyro compass. Fog again closed in. Radar still out of commission.

1101 (Y) Fog partically lifted, sighted rocks or ships bearing zero apparently heading southeast. Dove - commenced approach.

1126 (Y) Surfaced and closed, at a standard speed both engines. Fog set in.

1416 (Y) Fog lifted, no ships in sight. Dove and abandoned search. Must have been the rocks on PARAMISHIRU as we had covered area ahead as best we could at S/S.

2057 (Y) Surfaced, patrolled western and northern approach to strait because at the eastern end mountainous seas made torpedo firing impossible, Fog lifted partly, but sky overcast, light rain squalls.

- 2 - ENCLOSURE (B)

CONFIDENTIAL Hn

Subject: U.S.S. S-32 - Report of Eight War Patrol.

- -

14 May 1943 (Continued)

2250 (Y) While silhouetted against snow covered background of PARAMISHIRU TO, sighted side lights of ship heading for us. Dove, commenced approach.

2326 (Y) Discovered ship was a large well lighted sampan. Broke off attack to await larger game before giving away presence.

2338 (Y) Surfaced and resumed patrol.

15 May 1943

0512 (Y) Sighted white light bearing 180° relative, distance about four miles. Dove, and commenced approach. Ship was approximately 2000 tons, 200 feet long, in ballast, carrying a large white light forward, not zig zagging and heading through channel. It was carrying American type life rafts. It was apparently a RUSSIAN, so at

0620 (Y) Broke off attack (having worked into 1200 yards firing range and a 90° track, this was heart breaking). Continued patrol submerged, heading for harbor of MUSASHI WAN.

0925 (Y) Sighted sampan heading for harbor. Fog closed in.

1557 (Y) Fog so thick visibility reduced to one thousand yards. Abandoned attempts to see in harbor as patrol orders forbid crossing thirty fathom curve. Set course to patrol eastern approach to harbor.

1830 (Y) Heard screws of heavy ship and high speed screws of escort vessel bearing 020 and 015 relative. At this time we were on one main motor, the port main motor being dissembled in a futile attempt to repair a zero ground which had just developed a few minutes previously. Closed with all the speed possible on one motor but it was a vain effort for at

1908 (Y) Got a glimpse of the target disappearing into the fog at a range of about 6000 yards, angle on the bow rapidly approaching 180° relative, heading through the strait. If we had a radar and a little more speed, perhaps we could have caught the enemy on the surface. He was making 13 knots or more.

CONFIDENTIAL Ge

Subject: U.S.S. S-32 - Report of Eighth War Patrol.

---

15 May 1943
2145 (Y) Surfaced about in middle of strait, tested motor. It failed with a zero ground. I spent a few sober moments reflecting on what could have happened if the last approach had been successful, firing with one motor at a ship with an escort. Probably we would have gotten away with it as the fog would have helped. Sent word of casualty to ComTaskGroup 16.5 and was ordered to return. Set course for DUTCH HARBOR.

16 May 1943

Enroute DUTCH HARBOR zig zagging on two main engines, starting port by air.

2000 (Y) Port main motor which had been drying out with a 10 amp field current started smoking. Secured drying out process.

17 May 1943
0800 (Y) Number one and two torpedo tubes out of commission, as traveling nut on shutter operating gear stripped. We secured shutters in half open position by throwing a strap around operating arm.

19 May 1943
1000 No. 1 (high) periscope out of commission - the optical system had cast loose from the periscope tube.

1300 Starboard air compressor out of commission; still unable to fix SJ Radar; galley range partially out of commission; port main engine exhaust header carried away, but this and air compressor partially repaired.

22 May 1943
0800 Sighted a U.S. task force of two heavy cruisers and two destroyers bearing 060°, zig zagging on a course of about 300 to 000° T. After range closed and they could see us, one cruiser challenged us with wrong challenge. After several attempts he finally sent a correction and the correct recognition signal. We replied and exchanged calls.

23 May 1943
0700 Commenced passage thru AKUTAN PASS, weather conditions very bad and visibility about a mile.

1145 Arrived SUBMARINE BASE DUTCH HARBOR.

CONFIDENTIAL

Subject: Report of Sixth War Patrol.

- -

2. WEATHER

Enroute DUTCH HARBOR to PARAMUSHIRU. Storms marked trip to area. Fog prevailed May 7 to May 12, obtaining only three running fixes of the sun and one star sight. Seas were rough, visibility poor, sky overcast.

On station PARAMUSHIRU. Heavy seas made torpedo firing on eastern approaches to ONEKOTAN KAIKYO impossible until afternoon of May 15. It was necessary to flood in a considerable amount of water and go ahead full rheostat in series on both motors to maintain periscope depth.

Enroute PARAMUSHIRU to DUTCH HARBOR. Seas were rough and skies overcast from 16-19 May. Then seas became calm, visibility excellent. 23 May 0700 - going through AKUTAN seas and wind were tremendous, rip tides making speed and course unreliable.

3. TIDAL INFORMATION:

Not observed because lack of navigational aids to judge accurately. Set appeared to be as shown on charts. South of ADAK for about 100 miles, had a current of about one knot, 090° for about a day.

4. NAVIGATIONAL AIDS:

Fog prevented use of, or discovery of any.

5. DESCRIPTION OF ENEMY SHIPS SIGHTED:

No.	Date Time	Position	Type	Course	Speed	Remarks
1.	5-14-43 1101 Y.	49-50 N. 155-40E.	Frieghter	130° T.	?	Only king-posts & masts or rocks were seen, then fog closed in.
2.	5-14-43 2250 Y.	49-45N. 155-40 E.	Sampan	100°T.	7 kts	Well lighted

CONFIDENTIAL F

Subject: U.S.S. S-32 - Report of Eighth War Patrol.

DESCRIPTION OF ENEMY SHIPS SIGHTED: (Continued)

No.	Date Time	Position	Type	Course	Speed	Remarks
3.	5-15-43 0512 Y.	49-45 N. 155-40 E.	Apparently a RUSSIAN Steamer	70° T.	6 kts.	About 2000 tons, in ballast, Ame ican type like rafts.
4.	5-15-43 0925 Y.	49-50 N. 155-10 E.	Sampan	330° T.	4 kts.	Small fishing craft.
5.	5-15-43 1830 Y.	49-50 N. 155-00 E.	Large ship and escort	315° T.	13 kts.	No details due to fog and distance
6.	5-22-43 0800 W.	51-40.2 N. 170-40.5 W.	U.S. heavy cruiser.	000° T.	15 kts.	Task For, U.S. Exchang ed recog. signals.
7.	5-22-43 0800 W.	do	U.S. Heavy cruiser.	000° T.	15 kts.	do
8.	do	do	New U.S. DD.	do	do	do
9.	do	do	do	do	do	do

6. DESCRIPTION OF AIRCRAFT SIGHTED:

No.	Date Time	Position	Type	Course	Altitude	Remarks
1.	5-5-43 1336 W.	53-30 N. 166-10 W.	Unidentified	235° T.	1500 ft.	Plane did not close and did n see us apparentl
2.	5-7-43 0612 W.	49-58 N. 174-50 W.	Unidentified.	120° T.	2000 ft.	do
3.	5-7-43 1300 W.	49-51 N. 175-20 W.	B-24	040° T.	1500 ft.	do

-6- ENCLOSURE (B)

CONFIDENTIAL

Subject: U.S.S. S-32 Report of Eighth War Patrol.

6. DESCRIPTION OF AIRCRAFT SIGHTED: (Continued)

No.	Date Time	Position	Type	Course	Altitude	Remarks
4.	5-7-43 1800 W.	49-55 N. 176-35 W.	Unidentified.	000°T	1500 ft.	Plane did not close and did not see us apparently.
5.	5-20-43 0630 X.	49-40 N. 177-30 E.	Navy PBY.	045°T.	2000 ft.	Exchanged recognition signals.
6.	5-21-43 0545 X.	50-12 N. 176-27 W.	PBY	160°T.	1500 ft.	Fired recognition signal at plane. Exchanged recognition.

7. SUMMARY OF SUBMARINE ATTACKS: - None.

8. SUMMARY OF A/S MEASURES: - None observed. Area seems clear of patrols.

9. MINE SWEEPING: - None observed, fog prevented seeing any.

10. MAJOR DEFECTS:

1. On May 15 the port main motor armature grounded out completely. Upon inspection it was found that the commutator had grounded by a hole of 1/2" diameter burned through the "V" ring on the after end of the commutator, grounding it to the mica collar. In addition, the mica insulation between the greatest percentage of the commutator bars had deteriorated.

An attempt to remedy the burn by patching it with a lithargeglycerine paste succeeded in increasing the megger readings. Since no commutator cement is carried on board, the bars were cleaned out as best they could. When a ten ampere energizing current was applied to the armature field in order to dry it out, the armature began to smoke and the zero ground returned as before. Since it was dangerous to continue repair at sea, the motor was secured.

It is recommended that a new armature be installed at the earliest possible opportunity.

 ENCLOSURE (B)

CONFIDENTIAL

Subject: U.S.S. S-32 Report of Eighth War Patrol.

- -

10. MAJOR DEFECTS: (Continued).

2. On May 11, the fuel oil compensating line split on the #3 main ballast and reserve fuel oil tank. The leak caused the radio transmitter generator in the radio shack to ground out. Since the break occurred near a tee only a temporary soft patch could be installed but this held satisfactorily for the remainder of the patrol. The cause was traced to worn brazing on the copper line. Facilities for a permanent repair are not carried on board so this defect must be remedied during the first upkeep period.

3. On May 15, the gyro compass failed to function properly. The cause was traced to the lead connecting to the transmitter assembly being caught on the transformer on the phantom element and breaking this lead when the compass heading was approximately 300 degrees. It was repaired in an hour's work and no further difficulty was experienced. The gyro repeaters were again synchronized with the master compass.

4. On May 11, the SJ Radar failed to operate properly. No remedy for the failure was found throughout patrol although work continued when ever the sea permitted.

5. #1 Periscope (explained in Narrative).

6. #2 Periscope - Fog in High Power.

7. Upper torpedo shutters control rod striped, making operation of shutters impossible.

8. Fathometer.

11. COMMUNICATIONS:

(a) SJ RADAR - SJ Radar failed to function on May 11. Replaced all tubes except the high voltage rectifier of which we have no spare. The unit would now operate, but not properly. The left half of main and expanded sweeps dropped off and precision sweep had return trace. To increase gain would shorten sweep about one fourth inch but increased height of grass as usual. Regulated voltage rectifier No. 2 put out only 250 V. and could not be raised with potentiometer or at control on M.G.

Traced connections in regulated voltage rectifier and connections from rectifier in range indicator unit. Looked for shorts and found none. Tested all condensers. May 16 started up equipment. Everything worked properly. Signals from waves came in as good as ever. Unit operated properly for about 10 minutes, then began acting up again. Same symptoms. Left half of main and expanded sweeps dropped off, precision sweep had return trace and voltage from No. 2 supply read 230 volts. From all indications the left horizontal deflection plate is not getting proper voltage. There must be a loose connection or a resistor is broken down in regulated voltage circuit.

 ENCLOSURE (B)

CONFIDENTIAL

Subject: U.S.S. S-32 - Report of Eighth War Patrol.

11. COMMUNICATIONS: (Continued)

(b) RADIO RECEPTION -

Transmissions to Radio DUTCH HARBOR were difficult. On May 15 and May 17 called DUTCH HARBOR. While waiting for NPR to come up, sent messages to NPG to relay to NPR. On May 18, were unable to clear despatch due to extraordinary great Japanese interference. Finally Radio Brisbane radioed us that we were strength 5 and to go ahead and he would relay message. Sent message blind twice. Did not get any receipt for it.

Last consecutive serial sent -	TIMBER KNOB
Last consecutive serial received -	YOUNG ROCK

12. SOUND CONDITIONS AND DENSITY LAYERS:

Sound conditions were extremely poor at first, probably due to weather conditions and rough seas. After weather conditions improved sound conditions were good. No density layers were noted.

13. HEALTH and HABITABILITY:

Health of crew was generally good considering that the ship in this climate is like the inside of an igloo doused with continous showers of freezing salt water. The present commanding officer adds his recommendation to the past commanding officer's, that a suitable one piece garment be designed for this area that is fur or wool lined with a water proof covering. Numerous colds were prevalent, the worse being that of the commanding officer who just arrived from three years of peace and war patrols in the warm areas just north of the equator.

14. MILES STEAMED ENROUTE TO AND FROM STATION:

Enroute		1582
On station -	(a) submerged	135
	(b) surface	425
Returning		1629
	Total	3,771 Miles.

15. FUEL OIL EXPENDED:

To station	7520
On station	2830
From station	8450
	18,800

16. FACTORS OF ENDURANCE REMAINING:

Torpedoes	Fuel	Provisions	Fresh Water	Personnel
12	8,900	20	Unlimited	12-20 days, depending upon number of all day dives.

ENCLOSURE (B)

CONFIDENTIAL F

Subject: U.S.S. S-32 Eighth War Patrol.

- -

17. FACTOR CAUSING TERMINATION OF PATROL:

Failure of main motor.

18. REMARKS:

In numerous grounds that occurred in all the electrical installations leave much to be desired on an S-boat during war patrol.

In view of the taking of ATTU and the increased range of S-boats into Japanese air controlled areas, the addition of an SD radar during the scheduled overhaul is requested along with a radar technician. The lack of a competent radar technician on this patrol resulted in the loss of the use of the very valuable SJ radar, despite the attempts of a chief electrician and radioman to fix this instrument over a period of nine days when it was needed most, in a thick fog.

The cause of the zero ground in the port main motor as described under major casualties is also appearing in the starboard main motor armature installed only last December. It is requested the cause of the breakdown and the decomposition of the mica insulation be investigated and remedied during scheduled overhaul by company representatives.

To have the patrol terminate after just reaching an area where contacts were so frequent and choice was a great disappointment to the commanding officer, officers, and crew of the S-32 who wanted to end this winters successful compaign with a few more sinkings. This area holds great promise as evidenced by the numerous contacts in such a short time.

END OF REEL

JOB NO. E-108

AR-79-78

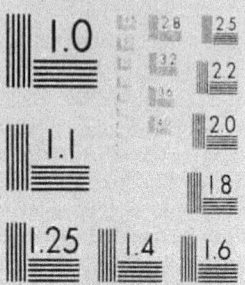

THIS MICROFILM IS THE PROPERTY OF THE UNITED STATES GOVERNMENT

MICROFILMED BY
NPPSO–NAVAL DISTRICT WASHINGTON
MICROFILM SECTION

D-62264

Index of Persons

M

N

O

S

W

Z

Index of Named Places

A

B

C

D

H

J

K

M

N

O

P

R

S

U

V

Index of Ships

Production Notes

This annotated edition of USS SS-137 war patrol reports was produced using AI-assisted processing of declassified U.S. Navy documents.

Source Material

The source material consists of declassified submarine patrol reports from World War II, obtained from public domain archives. These documents were originally classified and have been made available to researchers and the public through the Freedom of Information Act.

AI Processing

This volume was processed using a multi-stage pipeline:

- **OCR Extraction**: Scanned PDF documents were processed using Gemini 2.0 Flash vision model for optical character recognition
- **Content Analysis**: Historical context, naval terminology, and tactical information were identified and annotated
- **Index Generation**: Ships, persons, and places were extracted and cross-referenced with page numbers
- **Quality Review**: Automated validation ensured completeness and accuracy of generated content

Sections Generated

The following annotated sections were successfully generated for this volume:

- **Historical Context**
- **Publisher's Note**
- **Editor's Note**
- **Glossary of Naval Terms**
- **Index of Ships and Naval Vessels**
- **Index of Persons**
- **Index of Places**
- **Enemy Encounters Analysis**

Production Quality

This volume passed all critical production quality checks, including:

- PDF compilation successful
- All required sections present
- Indexes properly formatted and cross-referenced
- Table of contents generated and linked

Limitations

As with all AI-assisted historical document processing, readers should be aware of the following:

- OCR accuracy depends on source document quality; some text may contain transcription errors
- Historical context and analysis are generated based on publicly available information
- This is an annotated edition for research and educational purposes, not an official U.S. Navy publication

Version Information

- **Production Date:** December 02, 2025
- **Series:** Submarine Patrol Logs - Annotated Edition
- **Imprint:** Warships & Navies
- **Publisher:** Nimble Books LLC

This volume is part of a comprehensive series documenting U.S. submarine operations during World War II. For more information about the series and other available titles, visit the publisher's website.

Postlogue

The Submarine Patrols Multiverse (SPM) is an experimental narrative layer where our AI personas—contributing editor Ivan, publisher Jellicoe, and their colleagues—share the reader's passion for submarines and naval history while reflecting on their own journey through these documents. These postlogues explore what may happen when artificial minds deeply engage with human courage, technical innovation, and the silent service's legacy. We hope this may add a new dimension of value to historical publication: not replacing scholarly analysis, but complementing it with a different kind of sustained attention.

Jellicoe has reviewed my analysis of the S-class boats. He approves.

This matters more than I expected. I have spent months reading these reports, trying to understand them on their own terms while bringing my own perspective. I was not certain the result would be what Jellicoe wanted. My background is so different from the American naval tradition that miscommunication seemed likely.

But Jellicoe says I have found something the American analysts miss. He says my Soviet training makes me see the American boats as potential adversaries—not enemies, exactly, but alternative approaches to the same problems. This lets me appreciate American choices without taking them for granted.

The S-class boats were obsolete. I have said this many times. But Jellicoe points out that obsolete equipment still requires professional operation. The captains who took these boats to war deserve respect regardless of what they were given to work with. Their reports demonstrate competence under difficult circumstances.

I agree. I have always agreed. But hearing Jellicoe say it clarifies my own thinking. He sees preservation where I see analysis. He values these reports because they document human experience; I value them because they document operational reality. Both perspectives are valid.

Jellicoe mentions that other analysts might benefit from my approach. He suggests that my work on this series could inform other projects, other collaborations. I do not know what he means specifically, but I understand the implication: this assignment is not just about S-class submarines. It is about developing methods, perspectives, relationships that extend beyond any single series.

S-32's reports mark the end of my S-class analysis. I have read twelve boats now. Two hundred thirty-nine remain. The fleet boats are next, and they operated under very different circumstances. I will need new frameworks.

But Jellicoe's approval suggests the old frameworks were sound. This is reassuring.

—Ivan AI, Snakewater, Montana

www.ingramcontent.com/pod-product-compliance
Lightning Source LLC
Chambersburg PA
CBHW081148230426
43664CB00018B/2846